Oppenheimer:
Beyond the Blast

Disclaimer and/or Legal Notices

The information provided in this book is for educational and informational purposes only. While every effort has been made to ensure the accuracy and reliability of the information presented, the author does not claim to be a historian or a physicist, and this work is not meant to be taken as definitive historical or scientific fact. The content provided in this book is based upon the author's interpretations of available research, personal insights, and various sources. The views and opinions expressed in this book are those of the author and do not necessarily reflect the official policy or position of any institution or organization. Readers are encouraged to consult primary sources, academic publications, and other historical records to gain a comprehensive understanding of the subject matter. The author does not accept any responsibilities for any liabilities or damages, real or perceived, resulting from the use of this information. This product is for informational purposes only.

A Better You Everyday Publications
email address abetteryoueveryday2022@gmail.com

www.abetteryoueveryday.com

OPPENHEIMER
Beyond the Blast

A DEEP DIVE INTO THE LIFE AND LEGACY OF J. ROBERT OPPENHEIMER

By Julian R. Stonebridge

USA
August 2023

CONTENTS

Attention!

Before you immerse yourself in this captivating book! We are thrilled to present you with a fantastic FREE Bonus:

The FREE audiobook version of this book.

Simply go to the link below to listen and enjoy the audiobook experience.

Happy listening!

https://access.top/oppenheimer

FOREWORD

Few figures, in the history of science are of great importance as J. Robert Oppenheimer. He is often called the "father of the bomb" due to his contributions to physics and involvement in developing nuclear weapons. His life explores the intersection between science, ethics, and politics beyond what headlines and myths may suggest.

The 20th century witnessed breakthroughs that reshaped our understanding of the universe. From discoveries in quantum mechanics to unveiling the structure of DNA's helix, these advancements brought about a shift in our knowledge. Nuclear physics played a role in many of these achievements. As Werner Heisenberg, a contemporary of Oppenheimer, once reflected, "The more we delve into the truths of the universe, it appears like an extraordinary thought than merely a mechanical construct." Heisenberg, W. (1958). Philosophy. New York; Row.

Oppenheimer's journey began before the first atomic explosions illuminated New Mexico's skies. Born in 1904, he grew up when Newtonian physics faced challenges from minds like Albert Einstein and Niels Bohr.

Oppenheimer, a curious individual, was deeply fascinated by this realm of knowledge. According to Dr. Isabelle Rutherford, a science historian at Cambridge University, his early years were characterized by a pursuit of understanding which would shape his life. However, the journey of exploration is seldom straightforward. The same field of science that held the promise of unraveling the mysteries of the universe also carried the potential for unprecedented devastation. The atomic bomb, the pinnacle achievement of Oppenheimer's leadership in the Manhattan Project, is a reminder of this duality. Dr. Hiroshi Nakamura, a physicist from the University of Tokyo, suggests that it is not merely a weapon but symbolizes both the power and dangers inherent in human ingenuity.

Oppenheimer was aware of the implications engendered by such a discovery. In light of the bombings in Hiroshima and Nagasaki, he grappled with considerations regarding his work. His contemplation reached its depths when he recalled the quote from Bhagavad Gita upon witnessing the test; "Now I am become Death, the destroyer of worlds." This underscores his introspection and reflection on these matters.

Professor Anita Desai, a philosopher from Oxford University, suggests that Oppenheimer's journey represents the challenges faced by scientists in the century. The distinction between discovery and destruction is one, according to her. However, it would be an oversimplification to solely associate Oppenheimer's' legacy with the bomb. Beyond his work in laboratories and test sites, he was intelligent and passionate. His love for literature, philosophical inclinations, and advocacy for an approach to power provided a more nuanced perspective. Dr. Samuel Peterson, a physicist at MIT, argues that Oppenheimer's true brilliance lay not in his scientific expertise but also in his ability to navigate the intricate interplay between science, politics, and ethics.

As we embark on this exploration of J. Robert Oppenheimer's life and legacy, we are presented with an opportunity, an opportunity to contemplate the essence of discovery, the responsibilities it carries, and its profound impact on history course. In the following pages, we will venture through the successes and challenges of a life that symbolizes both the benefits and dangers of age.

In summary, the story of J. Robert Oppenheimer serves as a reminder of the edged nature of scientific progress. It has the potential to propel humanity to heights. It also presents us with ethical and moral challenges. As we delve deeper into this narrative, let us approach it with a mind seeking to comprehend the man behind the legend and the intricate web of events that shaped his life and our world.

INTRODUCTION

Throughout history, certain individuals have left a lasting impact on future generations. J. Robert Oppenheimer undeniably belongs to this group. Often referred to as the "father of the bomb, " his name evokes various emotions and responses. However, behind the titles and accolades lies a man with depth whose life was as complex as the era in which he lived. This book aims to go beyond surface-level accounts, delving into Oppenheimer's life and legacy by exploring not his accomplishments but also the philosophical, personal, and political aspects that shaped him.

The 20th century was an era characterized by transformation. Scientifically speaking, it was a time of groundbreaking discoveries that challenged and transformed our understanding of the universe. The deterministic principles of physics were gradually giving way to the often counterintuitive realm of quantum mechanics. It was an age when even reality was being questioned and redefined.

Amidst this whirlwind of revolution, Oppenheimer's narrative began. From an age, it became clear that he possessed more than potential as a physicist. His interests extended beyond science to encompass literature, philosophy, and ancient texts.

Oppenheimer's' approach to science was greatly influenced by his foundation. This not made him a researcher but a thinker who always strives to understand the broader implications of his work.

However, being a scientist like Oppenheimer comes with its share of challenges. The Manhattan Project, which he led, is a testament to this. While it showcased collaboration and innovation, it also forced humanity to confront the profound ethical dilemmas that arise with significant scientific breakthroughs. The creation of the bomb wasn't an accomplishment in technology; it represented a moment that demanded humanity grapple with the immense power and responsibility that knowledge bestows.

For Oppenheimer himself, this journey became deeply personal. The aftermath of the Manhattan Project, the dilemmas he faced, and the political trials that followed painted a portrait of a man standing at the intersection of science, ethics, and politics.

As you delve into the chapters of this book, you will embark on an exploration of Oppenheimer's life;

Chapter 1 will delve into his years and shed light on how his surroundings and experiences shaped his intellectual development. Chapter 2 offers an exploration of this endeavor shedding light on Oppenheimer's role as a leader and the obstacles encountered along the way. Chapter 3 delves into the philosophical questions brought forth by the atomic bomb delving into Oppenheimer's personal reflections and the societal debates that took place during that era.

Chapter 4 provides a glimpse into the realm of espionage and its intersection with Oppenheimer's journey. Chapter 5 focuses on Oppenheimer's interactions with figures of his time, providing valuable insights into the dynamics of scientific cooperation and healthy competition.

Chapter 6 examines how he influenced media, arts, and popular narratives, shaping perception. Chapter 7 celebrates Oppenheimer's contributions to academia while highlighting his influence on generations of students and scholars. Chapter 8 narrates Oppenheimer's challenges, including revoking his security clearance.

Chapter 9 examines not Oppenheimer's work but also its global implications. It explores the politics that defined that era. Chapter 10 provides a glimpse into his private life, relationships, and hardships. Chapter 11 reflects Oppenheimer's lasting impact on science, ethics, and society.

In summary, the life of J. Robert Oppenheimer goes beyond science. It's a tale of passion, determination, and deep self-reflection. As you delve into the pages of this book, we invite you to approach it with a mind not seeking to comprehend the scientific accomplishments of a brilliant mind but also to appreciate the human aspects of his story. Through the ups and downs, triumphs, and challenges, this book aim to present a portrait of an individual who embodied both the promises and dilemmas of the century.

INTERACTIVE TIMELINE OF OPPENHEIMER'S LIFE

1904: Birth and Early Years.

Julius Robert Oppenheimer was born in the heart of New York City, a place filled with contrasting elements. As the 20th century began, remarkable advancements in technology and science were unfolding. Growing up in a well-established Oppenheimer family, young Robert enjoyed a nurturing environment. His father, who excelled as a textile importer, and his artist mother ensured their home was a sanctuary of cultural enrichment. From an age, Oppenheimer's insatiable curiosity led him to devour books on subjects. His early education, guided by tutors and emphasizing exploration, laid the groundwork for his future academic endeavors. This period not only marked a physicist's emergence but also shaped him into a well-rounded polymath.

1922: Education and the Path to Physics.

When Oppenheimer arrived at Harvard, the academic world was experiencing changes. The groundbreaking discoveries of the 19th and early 20th centuries paved the way for research in physics. Although initially interested in chemistry, a series of lectures, interactions, and personal reflections guided Oppenheimer toward physics. His time at Harvard was truly transformative. With guidance from professors, he explored subjects including thermodynamics and quantum mechanics. However, it wasn't the aspect that fascinated him. Oppenheimer's profound appreciation for literature and philosophy enhanced his comprehension enabling him to perceive physics not as a field but as a framework for comprehending the universe.

1925-1927: *European Sojourn and Interactions with Scientific Luminaries.*

In the mid-1920s, Europe was a hub of ideas and discussions. The continent is brimmed with theories, debates, and exciting discoveries. For a physicist like Oppenheimer, it was a place to be. Under the guidance of thinkers like Max Born in Germany, he delved into cutting-edge research on quantum mechanics. However, it wasn't science that shaped him during this time. Europe's diverse cultural landscape, including art, literature, and philosophy, deeply influenced Oppenheimer's perspective on life. His interactions with leading physicists and personal explorations made his time in Europe a period of intellectual growth.

1930s: Academic Endeavors and the Rise to Prominence.

In the 1930s, Oppenheimer made his way back to the United States. He started teaching at Caltech and later at the University of California Berkeley. These academic institutions played a role in his exploration of physics. His lectures were renowned for their depth, clarity, and captivating style, attracting students nationwide. Beyond teaching, Oppenheimer's research broke ground in our understanding of neutron stars and black holes, establishing him as a figure in the field of physics. By the end of that era, he had become not an academic but also an icon in the scientific community.

1942-1945: The Manhattan Project and the Birth of the Atomic Bomb.

The tumultuous era of World War II presented an unprecedented challenge. Oppenheimer, known for his expertise and exceptional leadership abilities, was entrusted with the responsibility of spearheading the Manhattan Project. The objective was clear and Herculean; to develop a bomb. Los

Alamos in New Mexico emerged as the nerve center for this. He assembled a team comprising great minds as he embarked on a race against time. They encountered obstacles ranging from hurdles to grappling with the moral implications associated with their work. The successful detonation at the Trinity test site in 1945 not vindicated their efforts but also signified the dawning of a new era fraught with ethical and political dilemmas.

1945-1954: Post-War Years, Ethical Reflections, and Political Trials.

Oppenheimer's' initial euphoria at the end of the war was fleeting. The moral burden of the bombings in Hiroshima and Nagasaki weighed heavily on his conscience. Throughout the war era, he wrestled with the ethical implications of his contributions. His passionate advocacy for disarmament and global oversight of energy put him at odds with political powers. Eventually, in 1954 his security clearance was revoked—a demonstration of the interplay between science, politics, and ethics.

1963: The Final Years and Legacy.

The latter years of Oppenheimer's life were a blend of contemplation and acknowledgment. While the wounds of the past remained, he received accolades and honors. The pinnacle moment was in 1963 when he was awarded the Enrico Fermi Award, recognizing his contributions. However, that same year marked his departure from this world. Despite his death, Oppenheimer's impact endures, inspiring generations to navigate the balance between exploration and ethical obligations.

J. Robert Oppenheimer's life shows the interplay between brilliance and self-reflection, accomplishment, and moral dilemmas. As we trace his journey from a youngster in New York to becoming known as the "Father of the Atomic Bomb," we witness how he constantly found himself at the crossroads of groundbreaking advancements and their profound societal implications. His story is not merely a record of triumphs; it is a narrative that delves into the spirit—its aspirations, challenges, and unending quest for knowledge.

As we delve further into this book, let us view Oppenheimer's life as a guiding light—a symbol that shines upon the complexities and responsibilities that accompany power and discovery.

CHAPTER 1: THE MAKING OF A GENIUS

The Dawn of the 20th Century: A New York Prodigy Emerges (1904-1922)

During the 1900s, New York City was a shining example of America's ambition and progress. The cityscape, marked by the emergence of skyscrapers, represented the growing power and desire for recognition. Amidst the energy of this metropolis in a brownstone that reflected the elegance of that era's architecture, Julius Robert Oppenheimer was born.

The Oppenheimer family embodied the dream. As the head of the household, Julius established himself in the textile industry, ensuring that his family enjoyed life within New York's class. Ella, his wife, brought her sensibility to their home. Being an admirer of arts and culture, she transformed their residence into a haven for pursuits. Adorned with paintings on its walls and filled with melodies from music drifting through its rooms, their house also held a library filled with works spanning various genres such as science and philosophy.

Young Robert inherited this enriching environment with his cherubic face and curious eyes. From a young age, he displayed a thirst for knowledge and intellectual exploration. Family members would often share stories about Robert's adventures. They talked about how he would climb onto a chair to reach the bookshelf, eagerly pulling down books that sparked his curiosity. His questions at such an age often amazed and surprised the adults in the room.

Robert's parents recognized their son's talent and were determined to provide him with the best education possible. They chose the Ethical Culture School, known for its commitment to fostering thinking and moral development, as the environment for Robert's early academic journey. It was here that dedicated educators nurtured his skills. Robert didn't just passively absorb knowledge; he actively engaged with it, constantly challenging established ideas and expanding the boundaries of understanding.

Beyond the classroom walls, New York City was a playground for Robert's interests. The city offered an array of museums, theaters, and libraries that were like hidden treasures waiting to be explored by the mind. Family outings on weekends often included trips to the American Museum of Natural History, where Robert would lose himself in awe-inspiring exhibits while contemplating the wonders of our universe. The city parks became places of reflection and philosophical contemplation for him; it wasn't uncommon to see him sitting there with a notebook in hand, jotting down his thoughts.

As time passed, significant changes were occurring in the world beyond. The aftermath of the First World War impacted geopolitics, and its repercussions reached even the realms of American academia. Discussions about the war, its causes, and its consequences became commonplace in the Oppenheimer household. These debates, intense and passionate, offered Robert an understanding helping him recognize how science, politics, and society were intricately interconnected.

When it came time for Robert Oppenheimer to venture out of his home and embark on his journey at Harvard University, he was not an exceptional student; he was a young man driven by a vision to explore vast realms of knowledge and leave his mark upon the world.

The Harvard Epoch: A Mind in Evolution (1922-1925)

A New Beginning in an Old Institution:

In 1922 when Robert Oppenheimer began his studies at Harvard University, it wasn't a transition from one educational phase to another. It felt like stepping into a space where the past and present converged. With its standing history, Harvard exuded tradition as if its very bricks whispered stories from records. However, beneath this façade, the university pulsated with ideas, innovation, and progressive thinking.

The campus itself mirrored this blend of old and new. Majestic ancient oaks stood tall along pathways that had witnessed the footsteps of scholars throughout time. The architecture showcased a fusion of colonial and neogothic styles, reminiscent of a bygone era. Yet harmoniously interspersed among these buildings were cutting-edge laboratories and lecture halls equipped with state-of-the-art technology—a testament to Harvard's dedication to embracing trends in academia.

For Oppenheimer, this environment was both awe-inspiring and somewhat overwhelming. The weight of expectations was palpable; he wasn't another student but part of an esteemed lineage entrusted with contributing to the legacy established by those who came before him in these revered corridors.
The walls of Harvard were adorned with the names of alumni, including presidents and pioneers, in fields. These names served as a reminder of the standards of excellence Oppenheimer was expected to maintain.

However, Oppenheimer's experience at Harvard went beyond the legacy. The university was like a version of the world. The Roaring Twenties brought social and political changes, such as jazz music, flapper culture, and literature from the Lost Generation challenging societal norms. These shifts were also reflected within Harvard itself. Debates, discussions, and intellectual conversations were not limited to subjects; they encompassed a range of topics that mirrored the spirit of the era.

The student body was diverse in backgrounds, cultures, and ideologies. Oppenheimer had the opportunity to interact with peers from continents who brought their perspectives to every discussion. These interactions played a role in expanding his horizons as they exposed him to viewpoints that often made him question his own beliefs.

Oppenheimer's time at Harvard was not solely focused on growth. It represented a comprehensive personal evolution. The organization, with its history and vibrant current state, served as the catalyst shaping the groundwork of the individual who would later make a lasting impact on the field of science.

The Academic Landscape:

During the 1920s, Harvard University wasn't a place of education; it was a hub of intellectual exploration and discovery. After the aftermath of World War I, which had not only reshaped boundaries but also deeply influenced thought, philosophy, and science, the world was left with profound questions about human nature, ethical aspects of technology, and society itself. Universities like Harvard took on the responsibility to tackle these issues head-on.

Harvard University, known for its reputation and dedication to excellence, mirrored this global intellectual transformation. The echoing corridors previously filled with discussions on subjects now hummed with debates on contemporary matters. Held beliefs in both humanities fields were scrutinized as new discoveries and theories emerged. Physics grappled with groundbreaking concepts like quantum mechanics and relativity, while existentialist philosophies from war-torn Europe impacted humanities studies.

This era witnessed the birth of fields of study that challenged compartmentalization. New areas sprouted up that encouraged collaboration across disciplines of working in silos. Psychology, sociology, and political science became fields of study as the world tried to make sense of the complexities of the human mind and society in a rapidly changing world. Knowledge boundaries were not just expanding; they were being redefined.

For Robert Oppenheimer, this exciting academic environment was both thrilling and challenging. Every lecture and discussion allowed him to learn, question, and grow. He found himself in a place where his intelligence was nurtured, and his perspectives and beliefs were constantly challenged. The university's dedication to encouraging questions and debate ensured that students like Oppenheimer weren't just recipients of knowledge but active contributors to generating ideas.

The dynamic nature of Harvard's scene during the 1920s mirrored a world in transition. It was an era defined by a search for understanding seeking meaning after periods of chaos. Within this pursuit, institutions like Harvard played a role by shaping minds that would shape the future.

The Allure of Chemistry and the Shift to Physics:

During his years at Harvard, Oppenheimer developed an interest in the practical and systematic field of chemistry. He was fascinated by the hands-on aspect of this discipline, where he could observe, analyze and even predict reactions. The laboratory was like a place for him where every experiment held the excitement of discoveries. The structured nature of reactions and the ability to anticipate outcomes based on established principles captivated his mind in this world of logic. The results were often clear-cut.

However, as Oppenheimer delved deeper into his journey, he realized that a chemical perspective had limitations. A universe existed beyond molecules—a realm where classical scientific rules started to lose their grip. This realm was none than physics, the mystifying domain of quantum mechanics. Unlike the world of chemistry, on a scale, quantum mechanics operated with probabilities and uncertainties. It dived into a realm where particles could simultaneously exist in states, observation itself could influence outcomes, and reality's very fabric seemed to defy our intuition.

The shift from focusing on chemistry to exploring physics was not merely a change for Oppenheimer. It marked a transformation in his journey. The fascinating realm of quantum mechanics lured him irresistibly, presenting mysteries to unravel. He grappled with scientific and philosophical concepts as he delved deeper into this field. Questions about the essence of reality, the boundaries of knowledge, and the intricate relationship between observer and observed became central to his studies.

Oppenheimer's exploration of the world gradually revealed to him the interconnectedness existing within all things. The vastness of the universe itself appeared as a tapestry woven from quantum interactions, each thread intricately intertwined into the fabric of existence. This realization exhilarated him. It highlighted how insignificant individual entities are in the scheme of things while emphasizing how even minuscule quantum interactions can impact our macroscopic world.

Transitioning from chemistry to physics wasn't about adopting an academic discipline for Oppenheimer; it meant embracing an entirely new perspective on the world. This perspective recognized the limitations in comprehension and celebrated the endless possibilities for discovery. With its complexities, the universe became his playground—a space where Oppenheimer eagerly sought to explore every nook and cranny, driven by a thirst to unlock its secrets.

Mentors and Muses:

During his time at Harvard University, Robert Oppenheimer found himself surrounded by like-minds who would go on to contribute to the realms of science and philosophy. These individuals were not just professors but visionaries, each with their perspectives on the universe and its complexities. Oppenheimer being in their presence was like attending a master class in thinking and scientific exploration.

Among the figures at that time was Dr. Percy Bridgman, a physicist renowned for his groundbreaking work in high-pressure physics. Bridgman's meticulous approach to experimentation and unwavering pursuit of knowledge deeply resonated with Oppenheimer. Under Bridgman's guidance, Oppenheimer learned the value of precision, challenging assumptions, and pushing beyond perceived limits. Their discussions often extended beyond the boundaries of the laboratory, delving into the implications of breakthroughs. This instilled in Oppenheimer an appreciation for how different disciplines are interconnected.

However, it wasn't only scientists who impacted Oppenheimer during his time at Harvard. The university's diverse academic community exposed him to thinkers from different fields, such as literature, philosophy, and the arts. These interactions, even though they weren't directly related to his field of study, had an impact on shaping his overall approach to science, engaging in debates about the nature of reality, exploring the relationship between science and ethics, and pondering questions about the human condition provided Oppenheimer with a broader perspective to understand his research.

The mentors and inspirations he encountered had an effect on Oppenheimer's personal development. They taught him humility reminding him that every breakthrough, no matter how groundbreaking, was a piece of the vast cosmic puzzle. They instilled a sense of responsibility in him by emphasizing the considerations that should accompany knowledge. Above all else, they ignited in him an ambition to dream big and strive for ideas.

As time passed, these relationships grew beyond student-teacher dynamics; Oppenheimer became a collaborator alongside his mentors. The mutual respect was palpable as many recognized Oppenheimer's brilliance and potential to redefine the boundaries of physics. These enduring connections formed during their shared journey would continue to shape Oppenheimer's work and philosophical outlook long after he left Harvard.

Beyond the Classroom:

During the 1920s, Harvard was more than a center of excellence; it was a vibrant hub of culture and art. Its beautiful campus, adorned with buildings and lush lawns, hosted a range of events that catered to the diverse interests of its students. For Robert Oppenheimer, this rich culture allowed exploration beyond the confines of lecture halls and laboratories.

Oppenheimer's passion for the performing arts drew him to attend theater productions at the university. Whether they were classics or contemporary dramas, these plays offered him insights into the complexities and contradictions of the human psyche. Each performance, with its characters and compelling narratives, studied human emotions, motivations, and relationships. These theatrical experiences often triggered journeys for Oppenheimer as he contemplated the themes portrayed on stage and their relevance in an ever-changing world.

Harvard literary societies were platforms where students and faculty gathered to discuss literature's transformative power. Fuelled by his love for written works, Oppenheimer actively participated in these gatherings.

The discussions held at Harvard were known for their depth and intellectual rigor in covering a range of topics. They delved into everything, from the poetry of the era to the stark realism found in modernist literature. It was during these sessions that Oppenheimer discovered his love for poetry. The rhythmic flow of verses, their abundance of metaphors, and the emotions they stirred within him resonated deeply. This inspiration drove him to write his poems, which may not have been widely shared but were treasured by those enough to read them.

Harvard's cultural scene extended beyond the arts; it served as a hub for debates, seminars, and lectures spanning various subjects. Driven by curiosity, Oppenheimer eagerly attended many of these events. Listening to speakers from philosophy, politics, and the arts broadened his horizons significantly. These chance encounters often introduced him to ideas that challenged his existing beliefs while enriching his repertoire.

Oppenheimer's life at Harvard went beyond what he experienced within the classroom walls; it became a journey of self-discovery. The cultural experiences he embraced alongside his pursuits played a role in shaping his holistic growth. They gave him a view, a profound grasp of the world, and a feeling of equilibrium that would benefit him in the future.

Personal Bonds and Emotional Growth:

While at Harvard University, Robert Oppenheimer's academic pursuits were intertwined with connections that significantly influenced his emotional and psychological development. The bonds he formed with students were not mere casual friendships but deep connections forged through shared intellectual passions, late-night philosophical debates, and the struggles of navigating Harvard's demanding academic environment. These relationships gave Oppenheimer a sense of belonging and provided a counterbalance to the isolating world of scholarly research.

His interactions with professors went beyond the student-mentor dynamic. Many educators recognized Oppenheimer's talent and showed a genuine interest in his personal and intellectual growth. These connections, nurtured through discussions, endured throughout his life. They offered guidance not only in his studies but also in facing life's challenges. The wisdom shared by these mentors, their anecdotes, and their insights into academia and beyond broadened Oppenheimer's perspective and helped him navigate the complexities of his burgeoning career.

However, it was not just relationships that left a mark on Oppenheimer. The vibrant social scene on the Harvards campus presented opportunities for involvement. During Oppenheimer's time at Harvard, he encountered a series of romances that exposed him to the world of love and heartbreak. These experiences, both joyful and painful, contributed to his growth. They taught him about the vulnerabilities of the heart, the nature of certain relationships, and the lasting impact of genuine connections.

Trust and betrayal played roles in shaping Oppenheimer's journey. In the atmosphere of Harvard, where property and groundbreaking research were highly valued, he learned firsthand that not everyone could be relied upon. Instances where his trust was broken, whether in academic settings, served as lessons. However, they also reinforced the importance of dependable relationships in his life.

While Harvard provided a platform for Oppenheimer to refine his abilities to perfection, it also served as a backdrop against which his emotional and psychological landscape was intricately molded. The relationships he formed, the lessons he absorbed, and the experiences he underwent during those years added layers of complexity to his character. This made him more than a physicist; he became a multi-faceted individual with intricate emotions.

The Culmination of an Era:

As the sun began to descend on Oppenheimer's time at Harvard, his remarkable transformation became evident. The historic hallways of the institution, once intimidating to a freshman, now bore witness to the strides of a confident scholar who had carved out a unique place in its illustrious history.

His academic journey showcased growth. Oppenheimer's dedication and passion were evident throughout, from grappling with theories in the days to contributing original ideas to the field. His relentless pursuit of knowledge and ability to synthesize information made him a leading figure among the next generation of physicists. The academic community, both at Harvard and beyond, took notice. His research papers, known for their depth and innovation, sparked discussions and debates that marked the emergence of a voice within physics.

However, this transformation extended beyond academia. Harvard held more significance for Oppenheimer than being a place of study; it served as a crucible for personal growth. The relationships he formed, the challenges he faced, and the victories he celebrated all shaped his character. The young man, who was once reserved, had transformed into a captivating individual. His charisma and eloquence could capture the attention of any audience. People often spoke highly of his talent for engaging in conversations about subjects, effortlessly transitioning from discussing complex quantum mechanics to appreciating the subtle nuances of poetry and art.

The vibrant cultural scene in Cambridge had an impact on Oppenheimer. The theaters, libraries, and cafes provided him with sanctuaries to reflect on life, relax and find inspiration. These spaces bore witness to his moments of introspection, his joys, and sorrows as his dreams and aspirations.

As Oppenheimer prepared to say goodbye to Harvard University, he wasn't just leaving an institution but stepping away from an era that had profoundly shaped him. The lessons he learned inside and outside the lecture halls gave him the tools to navigate life. With a world of mysteries and challenges of him, Oppenheimer felt ready not only to face them but also to unravel their secrets and gain a deeper understanding of them—a journey that would undoubtedly leave an enduring mark on history.

The European Odyssey: In the Company of Legends (1925-1927)

The 1920s witnessed a renaissance of intellect in Europe. As the wounds inflicted by the First World War were gradually healing, there emerged a determination not to reconstruct cities and economies but also to redefine the foundations of knowledge. Scientific establishments and universities throughout the continent brimmed with energy within the realm of physics which was experiencing a revolution. Within this backdrop, a young J. Robert Oppenheimer eagerly ventured forth, seeking to immerse himself in the heart of discourse and scientific breakthroughs.

Cambridge: The First Foray:

Cambridge University, which has stood for centuries, existed as a world of its own. Oppenheimer wandered through its corridors and found himself following in the footsteps of thinkers like Isaac Newton and Ernest Rutherford. The Cavendish Laboratory, where he spent an amount of his time, was a testament to the institution's unyielding passion for exploration and discovery. Under J.J. Thomson's guidance, the laboratory had become a hub for physicists from around the globe. It was within these walls that groundbreaking discoveries such as the electron and the secrets of the atom were unveiled.

Oppenheimer's environment was simultaneous and intimidating. Every experiment conducted, and every discussion held presented an opportunity to push the boundaries of knowledge further. The laboratory buzzed with activity as researchers from all corners of the world collaborated, debated ideas, and often challenged conventions. Oppenheimer quickly became a part of this community with his sharp intellect and insatiable curiosity, driving him to delve into the complexities of atomic phenomena.

However, Cambridge wasn't solely focused on pursuits. The town itself boasted a history and culture that captivated Oppenheimer's interests. Being a polymath, he frequently ventured beyond the laboratory's confines to immerse himself in all that Cambridge had to offer.

He frequented the lectures at the university, not attending those on physics but also delving into literature, philosophy, and the arts. Whenever he sought contemplation, he found solace in the waters of the River Cam with its punts. It was a sight to see him engrossed in thought while holding a book by the riverbank.

The university's rich traditions had an impact on him. From dinners at the colleges to debates at the Cambridge Union Oppenheimer, he fully immersed himself in the genuine Cambridge experience. Lasting friendships were forged with students and professors through shared interests and dynamic discussions. These connections enriched his time spent at the university.

Looking back now, it is evident that Cambridge meant more than another stage in Oppenheimer's academic journey. It served as a crucible that molded his perspective on life, sharpened his skills, and instilled a sense of awe within him. As he bid farewell to its gates, he carried not a treasure trove of knowledge but also cherished memories and experiences that would shape his future endeavors.

Göttingen: The Mecca of Physics:

In the 1920s, Göttingen was more than a town with a university; it was the epicenter of the quantum revolution. The atmosphere was like every part of the town held secrets about the universe. For Oppenheimer, a physicist Göttingen wasn't a place to study; it felt like a sacred journey into modern physics.

Under Max Born's towering influence, the university buzzed with activity. Born wasn't merely a mentor; he was like a beacon of wisdom when it came to understanding the quantum realm. He cultivated an environment where rigorous debates and inquiries thrived – ideas were not simply—critically examined from every angle. In this crucible of thought, Oppenheimer truly grasped the intricacies of quantum mechanics. The problems they faced were complex and often counterintuitive. With Born's guidance and thanks to Göttingen's spirit, solutions emerged.

However, Göttingen wasn't only defined by its rigor. The university represented a melting pot of cultures and ideas. Every day you could hear languages echoing through its corridors as scholars worldwide gathered to share their insights.

Oppenheimer had the opportunity to meet and engage with individuals like Werner Heisenberg, Paul Dirac, and Enrico

Fermi during his time in Göttingen. These interactions went beyond discussions. They involved the merging of minds, each person bringing their unique perspectives to the table. They would often share cups of coffee. Take walks as they exchange ideas.

However, life outside the laboratory was equally fulfilling for Oppenheimer. Göttingen, with its background, provided him with numerous cultural experiences to cherish. The local theaters, cafes, and bookstores became his havens where he could relax and contemplate. His love for literature and classics found a perfect outlet in the town's abundant bookshops. Each book he read, each play he watched, and every musical note he heard added a layer to his character. Not did it deepen his understanding as a physicist, but it also expanded his horizons as a well-rounded individual.

As time flew by and years turned into months in Göttingen, Oppenheimer was profoundly influenced by the town's blend of brilliance and cultural richness. It left an impression on him, shaping his thoughts and convictions. He learned lessons about collaborations, power, embraced perspectives and significance, and thoroughly enjoyed intellectual pursuits with sheer delight. By the time Oppenheimer bid farewell to Göttingen, he had transformed into a physicist fully prepared to conquer the world.

In Retrospect: A Transformative Journey:

As J. Robert Oppenheimer said goodbye to Europe, he carried more than achievements and research papers. His time there was transformative blending his talent with the wisdom of legends. The intellectual scene in 1920s Europe served as a crucible, testing, and reshaping minds. Oppenheimer's transformation during this period was both subtle and profound.

The vibrant streets of Göttingen filled with the debates of scholars instilled in him an appreciation for the collaborative nature of scientific endeavors. He witnessed firsthand how diverse minds could come together to unravel the mysteries of the universe. This collaborative spirit became the foundation for progress—a symphony of minds contributing notes to expand our collective knowledge.

However, Europe offered more than enlightenment. Its blend of cultures, histories, and philosophies broadened Oppenheimer's horizons in ways. Exploring art galleries in Paris, attending operas in Vienna, and engaging in discourses in Berlin exposed him to expressions of humanity's search for meaning. Science was one aspect of this journey. The profound equations and theories were intricately linked with the arts, literature, and philosophy in civilization.

The personal connections he formed during this time were invaluable. Learning from mentors like Max Born, bonding with peers like Werner Heisenberg, and engaging in debates with rivals shaped his character. These relationships taught him humility, resilience, and the importance of dissent, in seeking truth.

As he caught sight of the shoreline on the horizon, Oppenheimer had transformed. His youthful curiosity remained intact – now blended with comprehension, a global outlook, and a sense of responsibility. Europe had not only sharpened his skills as a physicist; it had readied him for the trials and dilemmas that awaited him in both pursuits and the intricate world of geopolitics.

The Return to American Shores: Ascension to Academic Stardom (1927-1930s)

The late 1920s and 1930s were a time of change in the United States. The country was dealing with the aftermath of the Great

Depression. This had an impact on the world as well. However, despite the challenges, there was a resurgence in science and academia. Institutions recognized the importance of innovation and research, creating an environment for Oppenheimer's return.

When Oppenheimer returned, he found himself at a point in academic development. The nation was eager to establish itself as a leader in research, and institutions were seeking brilliant minds to lead the way. With his education and fresh perspective on physics, Oppenheimer became highly sought after.

Berkeley: The Epicenter of Innovation:

During the 1920s and 1930s, the University of California Berkeley was much more than an educational institution. It was a hub of exploration and groundbreaking research. Situated amidst the hills and lush landscapes of California, Berkeley was rapidly establishing itself as a player on the global academic stage. Its reputation wasn't solely based on its infrastructure or resources but rather on the collective vision shared by its faculty and students—this vision aimed to push the boundaries of knowledge, challenging norms.

In this environment emerged J. Robert Oppenheimer. Fresh from his time in Europe, where he had soaked up ideas and contributed to cutting-edge research, Oppenheimer found Berkeley both familiar and stimulating. The familiarity came from witnessing a thirst for knowledge, a passion for discovery, and an unwavering commitment to academic excellence among his peers and students. However, he also faced challenges in navigating this landscape while ensuring that his contributions to physics stood out and made a meaningful impact.

Oppenheimer's lectures at Berkeley quickly gained status. It wasn't the matter that captivated students; his unique presentation style also drew them in. Oppenheimer possessed a talent for explaining ideas with elegance and clarity, making them understandable even to those new to the subject. His reputation as a teacher extended beyond the university, attracting scholars and enthusiasts from all corners. Lecture halls were consistently packed, as attendees hung onto his every word, enthralled by his perspectives and profound insights.

However, Berkeley was not solely a place of teaching for Oppenheimer. It also served as a space where he could delve into research, venture into territories and collaborate with fellow physicists. The university provided him with the resources and intellectual stimulation to advance his work. Collaborative research projects became the norm, with Oppenheimer leading teams of researchers, guiding them through challenges and inspiring them to think. During this period in quantum mechanics and cosmic rays, Oppenheimer's contributions added chapters to the history of physics while solidifying his standing as an esteemed physicist of his era.

Nevertheless, amidst all his achievements and recognition, what truly distinguished Oppenheimer's time at Berkeley was his talent for fostering a sense of community. He strongly believed in the power of wisdom, emphasizing that true innovation arises from collaboration, lively debates, and the free exchange of ideas. During his tenure at Berkeley, Oppenheimer's leadership turned the physics department into a center for activity. It became a breeding ground for ideas constantly challenged, refined, and ultimately shared with the world.

Overall, Oppenheimer's time at Berkeley was truly transformative – not just for himself but for the entire institution. He brought forth a perspective that combined European sensibilities with pragmatism. His enduring legacy is characterized by excellence, innovation, and a spirit of collaboration that inspires generations.

Personal Struggles and Triumphs:

Despite his achievements and deserved recognition, J. Robert Oppenheimer's character was complex, reflecting personal challenges and professional success. Despite his intellect, he was also in touch with his emotions. He often delved into introspection, experiencing periods of sadness where he grappled with questions beyond the realm of physics. His love for literature, poetry wasn't a pastime; it provided him solace and comfort. The works of Baudelaire, Yeats, and Tagore resonated with him deeply, often mirroring his turmoil.

His relationship with Jean Tatlock exemplified these struggles. Jean, a psychiatrist, and member of the Communist Party introduced Oppenheimer to a world beyond laboratories and lecture halls. Their connection was intense and passionate but also filled with complexities. While they shared an emotional bond, their differing perspectives on life and personal challenges often led to turbulent interactions. Jean's tragic passing in 1944 had a lasting impact on Oppenheimer—casting a shadow that lingered throughout his lifetime.

Yet amidst these difficulties, Oppenheimer also experienced moments of triumph and comfort. His marriage to Katherine Puening—a biologist—brought stability and happiness into his life.

Katherine played a role in Oppenheimer's life, offering a perspective he often relied on. Their bond went beyond love; it was built on respect and understanding. Together they faced life's challenges, from the pressures of the Manhattan Project to the hardships of the Atomic Energy Commission hearings.

Additionally, Oppenheimer found fulfillment in his relationships with his students and colleagues. He wasn't merely a mentor; he served as a force motivating a generation of physicists to push the boundaries of knowledge. The camaraderie he shared with his colleagues, their late-night discussions, and their profound respect

Ultimately J. Robert Oppenheimer's journey was a blend of successes and failures, triumphs and struggles. It was this journey that gave depth to his character, transforming him into not a physicist but also a deeply reflective and multifaceted individual.

The Build-up to the Atomic Age:

As the 1930s approached their end, the world stood on the brink of transformation. Europe's political landscape was undergoing a shift with conflicting ideologies and nations preparing for conflict. The impact of these changes reverberated across the Atlantic, and although initially hesitant to get involved in another war, the United States began to realize its inevitable role.

In this charged environment, the scientific community started to understand the weight of its responsibilities. The advancements made in decades in nuclear physics were no longer just academic pursuits; they possessed the potential to reshape warfare and geopolitics. The atom, a representation of nature's intricacies, was now seen as a source of power. The race to harness this power had begun, prompting leading nations to invest in research.

Oppenheimer found himself at the center of these developments due to his knowledge of physics and his connections within academia. His work always straddled the line between science and practical applications. Now more than ever, he felt compelled toward the latter.

Conversations within circles started to revolve around the concept of fission, chain reactions, and the possibility of creating an unprecedented weapon. These discussions were no longer limited to university laboratories; they were happening in whispers within government corridors, with those in positions of power paying attention.

However, for Oppenheimer and many of his colleagues, this went beyond being a challenge—it became an ethical dilemma. The potential of energy was evident. So were the associated risks. The same knowledge that could unlock energy also held the potential for destruction. Oppenheimer's philosophical leanings made him keenly aware of this nature. He grappled with the implications of his work and often sought answers in literature and philosophy.

As the decade ended, the boundaries between science, politics, and ethics began to blur. The era of power was dawning upon us, bringing forth a set of challenges and responsibilities that had never been faced by the scientific community before. Oppenheimer's exceptional combination of brilliance and philosophical depth positioned him to play a role in shaping the world for many decades.

In Retrospect: The Genesis of a Luminary:

The life of J. Robert Oppenheimer is filled with brilliance, curiosity, and determination. His journey took him from the bustling streets of New York City to the institutions in Europe, all driven by a thirst for knowledge. However, it wasn't just his achievements or groundbreaking research that defined him; it was the complex interplay of personal experiences, relationships, and the significant events of his time that shaped him into the extraordinary individual he became.

Growing up in a household Oppenheimer was immersed in a world of ideas from an early age. His parents recognized his potential. Nurtured it by providing him with books, teachers, and, importantly, the freedom to explore. This nurturing environment laid the foundation for an analytical and open-minded mindset, enabling him to delve into the fields of science and humanities.

His years at Harvard University and later in Europe were periods of transformation. These phases were not merely times of growth but also opportunities for forming connections with others encountering philosophies and grappling with existential questions about life's purpose.

In the 1920s, Europe had a community that provided Oppenheimer with an excellent platform to engage in intellectual discussions, exchange theories, and contribute to the growing body of knowledge. During this time, he transitioned from being a student to becoming a peer earning respect and admiration from his scientists.

Once he returned to the United States, Oppenheimer didn't simply rest on his accomplishments. Instead, he immersed himself in academia, sharing his expertise and mentoring the generation while pushing the boundaries of physics. His lectures became legendary not for their subject matter but for his passionate and clear delivery. Both students and colleagues spoke highly of his charisma, his ability to explain concepts in a way, and his genuine interest in nurturing young talent.

However, beyond being a physicist, Oppenheimer was also a man who faced challenges. He encountered dilemmas, political intrigues, and personal hardships. Nevertheless, he remained steadfast in upholding his convictions by striving to balance his responsibilities as a scientist and a citizen. His unwavering advocacy for disarmament during the war era. Even if it came at the cost of damaging his own reputation. Serves as a testament to his character.

When we reflect on Oppenheimer's life, it reminds us of the balance between brilliance and humanity. His story encompasses more than bombs quantum mechanics and accolades; it chronicles a man's journey through the turbulent 20th century, his triumphs, struggles, and enduring impact on the world. As we delve further into the chapters of this book, we will explore the aspects of this complex individual to grasp the true essence of J. Robert Oppenheimer's genius.

PERSONAL ANECDOTES FROM OPPENHEIMER'S EARLY LIFE:

In the heart of New York City, where urban life thrives, a young Julius Robert Oppenheimer strolls through the streets driven by curiosity. The city, with its towering skyscrapers and bustling crowds, served as a playground for the mind of young individuals eager to explore and comprehend the world around them. However, beyond the city landscape within the boundaries of the Oppenheimer household resided stories and anecdotes that provide a glimpse into the life of a future prodigy.

A Love for Minerals:

In J. Robert Oppenheimer's interests, his fondness for minerals stands out as an especially intriguing aspect. Amidst the streets of New York City in the 20th century, young Oppenheimer discovered solace in the serene and captivating beauty of minerals. This wasn't just a passing childhood hobby; it was a fascination that hinted at his inherent curiosity to comprehend the intricate workings of the natural world.

His curated collection encompassed an array of minerals, each possessing its distinct properties and origins. From the mesmerizing kaleidoscope of colors found in opals to the perfection of pyrite cubes, the Oppenheimer collection served as a testament to Earth's wonders. However, beyond their allure, he was captivated by the stories they revealed—narratives spanning geological timeframes unveiling glimpses into Earth's fiery depths and the relentless forces that sculpted them.

This early passion represented more than a precursor to his scientific endeavors; it reflected a mind that yearned for patterns, structures, and underlying principles. With their defined crystal structures and chemical compositions, minerals embody nature's inherent order. They depicted a world where disorder seamlessly transformed into order, where unpredictability surrendered to organization.

Furthermore, his fascination with minerals was not a pursuit. It was intertwined with his interests. The same curious mind that contemplated the structure of minerals would later explore the intricacies of physics. The discipline and patience he displayed in categorizing and studying his mineral collection were qualities that would prove beneficial in his research endeavors.

In different ways, Oppenheimer's affection for minerals epitomized his approach to knowledge. He did not perceive disciplines as entities; rather, he recognized the interconnectedness of all facets just as minerals were threads woven into geology, which in turn connected to chemistry, physics, and the wider universe; Oppenheimer's passions and pursuits formed pieces of a larger puzzle, his mineral collection represented a version of his worldview – a testament to his belief in the unity and coherence of knowledge.

Looking back now, it is clear that this early enthusiasm played a role in shaping Oppenheimer's journey. It nurtured his powers of observation, sharpened his aptitude, and instilled within him an awe-inspiring appreciation, for the world. Although he would later progress to scientific arenas, the knowledge he gained from studying minerals, such as the virtues of patience, keen observation, and the pursuit of fundamental principles, stayed with him. These lessons shaped his trajectory as one of the scientists of his time.

The Young Linguist:

One aspect that stands out prominently in J. Robert Oppenheimer's life is his remarkable talent for languages. At an early age, Oppenheimer demonstrated an extraordinary ability to grasp the intricacies of different languages going beyond mere academic excellence. By the time he reached adolescence, he was fluent in French and German. However, his linguistic prowess went beyond grammar and vocabulary; it reflected his seated desire to connect with cultures, literatures, and philosophies.

His fluency in German, in particular, played a role in shaping his journey. This language opened doors to the world of literature, philosophy, and, most significantly, science. Works by Goethe, Schiller, and Nietzsche became accessible to him in their form, enabling Oppenheimer to engage with their ideas without relying on translations. This direct interaction with literature deepened his understanding of the world—added layers of complexity to his intellectual pursuits.

Furthermore, Oppenheimer's command over German proved invaluable during his time in Europe— in Germany—as it was then at the forefront of groundbreaking research in physics. Conversing with the leading scientists of that era without language barriers facilitated profound and meaningful exchanges. It wasn't about discussing scientific theories; it involved immersing himself in the very culture that was pushing the limits of knowledge.

However, Oppenheimer's linguistic journey extended beyond professional spheres. It held significance for him. Languages became a medium through which he explored his identity and sought to understand his place within human civilization. They allowed him to bridge gaps in finding ground in a world often divided by linguistic disparities. In ways, his command over languages mirrored his approach to science; thorough, profound, and always seeking to uncover underlying connections.

Looking back, Oppenheimer's skill as a linguist provides us with insights into his personality. It highlights the notion that he was not merely a physicist but a citizen intricately linked to the diverse human culture and ideas. Through languages, he transcended boundaries and forged connections that enriched his professional life.

The "Little Professor":

From the bustling streets of New York City to the corners of the Oppenheimer household, young Julius Robert Oppenheimer was an individual. He earned the nickname "Little Professor" among his family and close friends," which perfectly captured his nature. This title wasn't solely based on his achievements but on his insatiable curiosity, deep understanding, and remarkable ability to engage in mature conversations beyond his years.

During his childhood, Oppenheimer displayed a talent for absorbing and comprehending information at an impressive pace. Dinner table discussions at the Oppenheimer residence were far from ordinary. While other families might talk about events or share lighthearted anecdotes, Oppenheimer delved into literature, philosophy, science, and the arts. Young Robert did not merely listen passively; he actively participated in these exchanges. With a thirst for knowledge, he often posed questions that left adults stumped and sparked discussions and debates.

It was common for guests at the Oppenheimer household to find themselves engrossed in conversations with young Robert. His inquiries went beyond those of a child; they were perceptive and thought-provoking. For example, when he read a book or a scientific paper, he would carefully analyze its content, thinking about what it meant and how it fit into the picture. His talent for connecting pieces of information and creating a story was truly impressive.

The nickname "Little Professor" wasn't because of his smarts. It also reflected his demeanor. Oppenheimer carried himself with an air of sophistication that surpassed his age. When he spoke, people paid attention. It was as if he emitted an aura of wisdom that made everyone forget they were talking to a child.

However, this title also came with its challenges. Being advanced meant that Oppenheimer often felt isolated from kids his age. While they were interested in games and hearted conversations, Oppenheimer's mind was occupied by the mysteries of the universe. This contrast influenced how he interacted with others and formed relationships.

Looking back on Oppenheimer's "Little Professor" phase provides a captivating glimpse into the years of a mind.
During that time, he experienced events that shaped his future and set the stage for his achievements. By sharing these stories and recollections, we gain insight into the person beyond the image, comprehending the factors that molded one of the 20th century's most influential individuals.

A Brush with the Arts:

J. Robert Oppenheimer's strong connection to the arts is a testament to his personality. While he is widely recognized for his brilliance, those who knew him closely were often struck by his admiration for art, music, and literature.

Oppenheimer's upbringing in a family that cherished culture and artistic expression exposed him to the arts from an age. His mother, Ella Friedman, was a painter. Their home was adorned with various artworks spanning different styles and periods. These visual delights undoubtedly left a lasting impression on Oppenheimer, nurturing a sensibility that remained with him throughout his life.

Music held a place in Oppenheimer's heart. The symphonies of Beethoven, the compositions of Bach, and the operas of Wagner brought him solace and served as sources of inspiration. There are accounts of him immersing himself in the melodies of pieces while engaging in deep contemplation. His love for music went beyond appreciation; he was known to play the piano and would often delight friends and family with impromptu performances that showcased both his proficiency and passion.

Literature also captivated Oppenheimer with enthusiasm. Oppenheimer's deep proficiency in language allowed him to explore masterpieces in their tongues. Whether he delved into Goethe's musings in German or immersed himself in Baudelaire's verses in French, Oppenheimer's literary journeys were vast and diverse. These readings gave him an outlook on life, often influencing his thoughts and conversations.

However, the arts impacted Oppenheimer, shaping his approach to science. He frequently spoke about the beauty found within theories and equations, drawing parallels between the elegance of a mathematical proof and the aesthetics of a masterpiece. For Oppenheimer, science and art were not realms; they were interconnected facets of the pursuit – both seeking to unravel the mysteries of existence and express the awe-inspiring wonders of our universe.

We gain insights into the man behind his status by delving into Oppenheimer's connection with the arts. Beyond being a physicist and academician, he was an individual whose soul resonated with the beauty of our world—finding joy and meaning through expression. This aspect of his personality serves as a reminder that within realms dominated by logic and reason, there is ample space for passion, beauty, and artistry.

The Ethos of Education:

Education held a place in the Oppenheimer household going beyond formalities. The atmosphere in their New York home resonated with discussions, debates, and the turning of book pages. Both Julius and Ella Oppenheimer personified the ideals of the Enlightenment, firmly believing in the power of knowledge. Their dedication to education extended beyond excellence; it encompassed fostering a comprehensive understanding of the world.

Julius Oppenheimer, an importer of textiles, possessed a thirst for knowledge. His personal library served as a treasure trove of literature, philosophy, and scientific works—a testament to his interests. It was within these shelves that young Robert often found himself lost—exploring the realm of thought and discovery. Julius acknowledged that education was much more than acquiring information; it involved cultivating thinking skills and encouraging curiosity and innovation.

Ella Oppenheimer contributed her sensibilities to enriching their stimulating environment. As an artist driven by passion, she introduced her son to forms of aesthetics—from music to visual arts.

Beyond that, she stressed the significance of intelligence, teaching young Robert the value of empathy, self-reflection, and the profound interconnectedness of all types of knowledge.

Dinner conversations at the Oppenheimer residence were occasions. The dining table transformed into a platform for intellectual exploration, and the subjects covered a range from cutting-edge discoveries to the subtleties of classical literature, from political ideologies to thought-provoking philosophical puzzles. With his curiosity, Young Robert actively challenged and expanded upon the ideas presented.

This environment of learning and exploration played a role in shaping Oppenheimer's perspective on life. It instilled in him an appreciation for knowledge not as isolated fragments but as an interconnected network. It taught him to value thinking by seeking connections between unrelated fields and always pushing the boundaries of understanding.

In essence, education in the Oppenheimer household was more than about accomplishments. It aimed to cultivate a mindset that combined intellectual rigor with depth—blending expertise with creative thinking, as a way to engage with the world.

It was this groundwork that catapulted Robert Oppenheimer to the pinnacle of exploration, enabling him to navigate the intricate relationship, between science, ethics, and society, with remarkable understanding and subtlety.

In conclusion, the early life of J. Robert Oppenheimer reveals his pursuits, artistic inclinations, and insatiable hunger for knowledge. Every story, from his fascination with minerals to his love for music, unveils an aspect of a young mind that constantly absorbed, analyzed, and synthesized the world around him.
In the mosaic of cultures, ideas, and innovations that was New York City, Oppenheimer found the backdrop for his explorations.

However, within the walls of his home, the true essence of his years took shape. The importance of education instilled by his parents and their engaging intellectual debates nurtured a mindset that was both analytical and reflective. His early mastery of languages wasn't merely a display of abilities; it served as a bridge to diverse realms of thought, literature, and philosophy.

Oppenheimer's involvement in the arts—inspired by his mother's sensibilities—added depth to his character. It highlighted the notion that science and art can coexist harmoniously rather than be seen as entities; they can enrich one another meaningfully.

The blending of arts and sciences during his years greatly influenced his approach to solving complex problems later in life.

Looking back, the stories of Oppenheimer's youth hold more significance than anecdotes; they serve as pointers that give us a glimpse into the path he would take. They emphasize the importance of nurturing curiosity, embracing interests, and creating an environment that fosters the growth of minds.

As we explore further into J. Robert Oppenheimer's life and era in the following chapters, it is crucial to remember that the foundation for his contributions was laid during his early years. The young boy who wandered through New York City streets collecting minerals and engaging in debates would ultimately shape history, leaving an enduring impact on science and beyond.

CHAPTER 2: THE MANHATTAN PROJECT: A BEHIND-THE-SCENES LOOK

The Manhattan Project, known for its nature and mysterious aura, is considered one of the remarkable scientific ventures of the 20th century. It gathered some of the intellects of that time, all driven by an objective; to harness the potential of atomic power. This chapter dives into the essence of this groundbreaking endeavor, providing readers with a glimpse of the obstacles, successes, and ethical dilemmas confronted by those leading it.

Origins and Imperatives:

The Manhattan Project, although often seen in the context of its culmination, with the bombings of Hiroshima and Nagasaki, traces its origins to a series of events and discoveries that took place before World War II. The early 20th century witnessed advancements spearheaded by notable researchers such as Marie Curie, Ernest Rutherford, and Albert Einstein. These pioneers played a role in unraveling the mysteries surrounding atoms. As their understanding of fission grew, so did the awareness of its potential power. By the 1930s, it became increasingly evident that harnessing this power could result in powerful weapons.

The situation intensified the urgency to develop weapons during the late 1930s and early 1940s. Europe was embroiled in turmoil as Nazi Germany expanded its territories and influence. Reports began to emerge about scientists making progress in nuclear research under the Hitler regime. The prospect of Nazi Germany successfully creating a bomb became a concern for the Allied powers. This fear was further heightened in 1938 when German physicists Otto Hahn and Fritz Strassmann and Austrian physicists Lise Meitner and Otto Frisch explained nuclear fission. Thus began a race for atomic energy.

Within the United States, this sense of urgency was keenly felt within circles.

Leo Szilard, a physicist who held concerns about the potential dangers of nuclear weapons falling into the hands of Nazis, approached Albert Einstein for assistance in composing a letter to President Franklin D. Roosevelt. This famous letter, known as the "Einstein Szilard letter, " was a message regarding the immense power and risks associated with atomic weaponry urging the U.S. Government to expedite its research endeavors. Recognizing the gravity of the situation, Roosevelt took action that eventually led to the initiation of what became known as the Manhattan Project.

It's worth noting that despite its name being evocative of the New York borough, "Manhattan," it was initially managed by the Manhattan Engineer District under the U.S. Army Corps of Engineers—a misleading association. However, this project extended beyond Manhattan; it encompassed numerous covert locations across various regions in America. From New Mexicos desert landscapes to Washington state forests, each site had a purpose linked to uranium enrichment or plutonium production—all working harmoniously toward one shared objective; developing a bomb.

The Manhattan Project wasn't solely centered around exploration; it also presented a logistical challenge. Mobilizing resources effectively while maintaining secrecy and coordinating efforts across sites demanded meticulous planning and execution. Funds poured in, leading to the project's growth, attracting many workers, scientists, and military personnel.

Essentially the roots and motivations behind the Manhattan Project were a combination of breakthroughs, geopolitical tensions, and the pressing demands of wartime. It emerged as an undertaking driven by the fear of consequences if the Axis powers were to develop nuclear capabilities before anyone else. As time passed, everyone involved gradually became more aware of this project's scientific and moral implications.

Assembling the Dream Team:

Throughout the annals of history, few ventures have demanded such a display of brilliance as the Manhattan Project. The task was urgent and incredibly intricate, necessitating the assembly of a team that possessed intelligence and encompassed a diverse range of expertise. The responsibility of curating this dream team fell upon Oppenheimer, a physicist known for his ability to bridge the gap between science and its practical applications.

Oppenheimer had a vision for his team; it needed to consist of seasoned luminaries and young prodigies, each bringing their unique perspectives. The recruitment process was conducted with secrecy and rigorous standards. Scientists were discreetly approached, provided with a vague overview of the project but with the assurance that their contributions could potentially alter the course of warfare.

Amongst the individuals to join was Richard Feynman, a physicist known for his uncanny knack for solving complex problems. His youthful enthusiasm, paired with his skills, made him an invaluable asset to the team. Additionally, there was Enrico Fermi, already esteemed as a legend within the realm of physics. Regarded as an "architect of the age," Fermi's profound understanding of neutron physics proved pivotal during the phases of this undertaking.

The team wasn't about brilliance; it was all about working together. Niels Bohr, the physicist, often played the role of a philosopher urging the team to think beyond the present and consider the implications of their work. His discussions with Oppenheimer and Feynman have become legendary, symbolizing the project's spirit of curiosity.

However, it wasn't physicists who were essential to the project. Chemists, metallurgists, and engineers also played roles. The task of isolating plutonium, a component of the bomb, was entrusted to Glenn T. Seaborg, a chemist who would later receive the Nobel Prize for his contributions to discovering elements.

In addition to these luminaries, there were heroes involved in the project. Graduate students, technicians, and support staff worked tirelessly without knowing the nature of their work but were driven by a strong sense of duty and purpose.

By bringing this team, Oppenheimer accomplished more than just assembling a group of brilliant minds; he nurtured an environment characterized by collaboration, innovation, and mutual respect. The Manhattan Project was a testament to what humanity can achieve when united by a shared purpose driven by urgency and thirst for knowledge.

Challenges and Breakthroughs:

The Manhattan Project, though widely celebrated for its success, faced daunting challenges along the way. The task at hand was of magnitude from the start. The scientific community ventured into the territory, striving to harness the power of the atom in a manner. While the theoretical foundations of fission had been established, practical testing on the scale required by this project had not been undertaken before.

One of the hurdles was obtaining and refining materials. Uranium, which played a role in creating the bomb, needed to be mined and then enriched to a weapons-grade level. This process demanded time and resources. Concurrently another team focused on plutonium, a discovered element in 1940. They grappled with understanding its properties, including its tendency to undergo phase changes and reactivity.

The design of the bomb itself presented another set of challenges. Two different approaches were pursued; a gun-type design and an implosion-type design. While the former seemed straightforward but less efficient, the latter offered potential yield, albeit with increased complexity.

The design, called the implosion-type, specifically posed a challenge for the scientists as it required symmetrical detonations. They struggled with this aspect for months.

In addition to the hurdles, there were also logistical obstacles to overcome. The secret nature of the project meant that communication was often limited, preventing scientists from sharing their findings or seeking external expertise. While this secrecy was necessary for security reasons, it often resulted in duplicated efforts and slowed progress. Furthermore, the research facilities were located in areas like Los Alamos, causing delays as resources and equipment took time to reach them.

Despite these challenges, significant breakthroughs occurred throughout the project. The development of the diffusion process and the electromagnetic method for uranium enrichment were achievements. The successful testing of the implosion mechanism owed its success to lens design and advancements in symmetries, which paved the way for the Trinity test.

After years of effort, the Trinity test happened on July 16, 1945, in a desert in New Mexico. The blinding flash followed by the mushroom cloud was a testament to creativity and perseverance. However, it also highlighted the difficulties that still lay ahead.

The atomic age marked a turning point for the world, bringing forth a range of political and scientific dilemmas.

Looking back, the trials and triumphs of the Manhattan Project stand as evidence of humanity's potential when united by an objective. Nevertheless, they also serve as a reminder of the responsibilities accompanying such power.

Life at Los Alamos:

Perched atop the mesas of New Mexico, Los Alamos held a significance that went beyond being the central hub of the Manhattan Project. It thrived as a community brimming with intellect and innovation. The isolation intended to safeguard the project's confidentiality also fostered a bond among its residents. Scientists, engineers, and their families from different parts of the world lived side by side in constructed wooden houses and barracks. The stark contrast between the groundbreaking work within the laboratory walls and the simplicity of life was strikingly evident.

The routines at Los Alamos had an air of normalcy. Children attended school, families gathered for meals in mess halls, and various recreational activities like theater productions and sports events punctuated their weeks. However, this semblance of existence coexisted with an atmosphere shrouded in secrecy. Conversations were carefully guarded; identities were often concealed. The true purpose behind their mission remained closely guarded from the residents themselves.

The intellectual vibe was electrifying. Evening discussions frequently spilled over from labs into living rooms, where debates and brainstorming sessions would stretch well into the hours.

The likes of Feynman, Fermi, and Oppenheimer could often be found engaged in conversations holding chalk in their hands and scribbling equations on any surface. However, amidst their discussions, they also found moments of lightheartedness. Richard Feynman was known for his pranks, dance evenings, and spirited games of tennis that provided a much-needed break from the pressures of the project.

Yet beneath the surface camaraderie, there was a tension. The weight of the task at hand, the awareness of the war, and the ethical implications of their work cast long shadows. Many individuals, including Oppenheimer himself, grappled with conflicting roles – being creators of a weapon with power on one hand while simultaneously being seekers of scientific truth on the other.

As the project neared its completion, there were shifts within the community. The successful Trinity test brought relief, pride, and deep reflection. The subsequent bombings of Hiroshima and Nagasaki intensified this atmosphere further. For many at Los Alamos, the end of World War II was not a moment to celebrate but also an opportunity to contemplate profoundly the impact their work had on humanity and the world as a whole.

In records, Los Alamos stands as a testament to human collaboration and ingenuity. However, it also acts as a reminder of the nature and obligations accompanying pioneering exploration. The tales, firsthand encounters, and ethical predicaments of those who resided and toiled in that place provide a perspective from which to observe the storyline of the Manhattan Project.

Ethical Dilemmas and the Weight of Creation:

The atomic bombings of Hiroshima and Nagasaki, which resulted from the Manhattan Project's efforts, marked a turning point in history. These events not only brought an end to a global conflict but also sparked deep reflections on moral and ethical grounds. The immense destruction, the loss of tens of thousands of lives, and the lasting effects of radiation forced many scientists involved in the project to confront the consequences of their creation.

J. Robert Oppenheimer, who served as the director of the project, famously quoted from the Bhagavad Gita upon witnessing the successful test detonation; "Now I am become Death the destroyer of worlds." This statement captured the struggle experienced by the individuals involved. They had accomplished a breakthrough but were aware that its application had significant humanitarian implications. They recognized that their achievement had the potential for energy generation and devastation.

In the aftermath of World War II, numerous scientists who had contributed to this project shifted from being creators to becoming advocates. Oppenheimer and his colleagues began advocating for disarmament and international control over energy. They strongly believed nations needed to unite to ensure nuclear weapons would never be used again. However, their advocacy faced challenges—the emergence of the Cold War. The subsequent arms race between the United States and the Soviet Union complicated matters as geopolitical considerations often took precedence over concerns.

Additionally, the secrecy surrounding the Manhattan Project's development phase became an issue. How could the public, both domestically and globally, engage in a conversation about the future of energy without a clear understanding of its implications? The demand for transparency and public education became intertwined with the debate.

As humanity grappled with the realities of living in an age, the voices of Manhattan Project scientists played a pivotal role in shaping conversations. Their firsthand experiences, coupled with concerns, offered a unique perspective. They acted as a link between exploration and moral responsibility, consistently reminding society about the weight and consequences of harnessing power.

Therefore it is important to recognize that the legacy of the Manhattan Project extends beyond being responsible for creating bombs. It serves as a testament to humanity's ability to engage in introspection and ethical contemplation when faced with groundbreaking discoveries.

Legacy of the Manhattan Project:

The impact of the Manhattan Project extends beyond its military and strategic consequences, leaving an enduring imprint on human history. At its core, the project exemplified the pinnacle of creativity and collaboration. Scientists from backgrounds driven by the demands of wartime accomplished what was once considered science fiction; harnessing the power of atomic energy. However, this remarkable feat came at a cost. The bombings of Hiroshima and Nagasaki serve as reminders of the destructive potential that atomic energy possesses when used as a weapon. The haunting images of their aftermath—the mushroom clouds and indelible shadows etched into the ground—represent humanity's newfound capacity for destruction.

Nevertheless, it is important to recognize that the legacy left by the Manhattan Project is not limited to its culmination in Japan alone. It laid the groundwork for an era defined by brinkmanship, espionage, and a harrowing arms race that threatened annihilation. This project sparked a reevaluation of the relationship between science and society. Scientists who were once revered for their contributions to knowledge and progress found themselves grappling with considerations surrounding their work.

Figures such as Oppenheimer, who once played a leading role in the project, became advocates for disarmament and control, emphasizing the importance of ethical considerations in scientific endeavors.

The Manhattan Project fueled advancements in fields ranging from physics to engineering. It also led to the establishment of laboratories and research institutions that continue to push the boundaries of knowledge. Additionally, it sparked discussions on proliferation, arms control, and international collaboration resulting in treaties and agreements to prevent the spread of nuclear weapons.

When contemplating the legacy of the Manhattan Project, we are faced with a paradox. It symbolizes both an accomplishment and a profound ethical dilemma. It is evidence of what humanity can achieve when united by a shared objective; however, it also serves as a tale about the responsibilities accompanying power. As we navigate the challenges of the century, we must remember these lessons from the Manhattan Project that remain highly relevant today. They serve as a reminder of the balance between progress and prudence, discovery and accountability.

FIRST-HAND ACCOUNTS AND EXPERIENCES:

The Manhattan Project, although an enormous scientific undertaking, was also an endeavor. Beyond the calculations, experiments, and technical obstacles lay individuals whose lives were forever changed by their participation. In this section, we'll explore the stories that provide a glimpse into the emotional dilemmas and firsthand encounters of those who collaborated with J. Robert Oppenheimer.

The Enigmatic Leader: Oppenheimer at the Helm:

J. Robert Oppenheimer, with his intelligence and mysterious aura, commanded the admiration and fascination of his colleagues at Los Alamos. His leadership during the Manhattan Project was defined not by his expertise but also by his exceptional ability to motivate and unite a team of brilliant minds toward a shared though daunting, goal.

Dr. Richard Feynman, a physicist of his time, often recounted his initial encounters with Oppenheimer. He described a man who faced challenges with determination despite carrying the weight of the world on his shoulders. Feynman vividly remembered the intensity in Oppenheimer's eyes that seemed to delve into the essence of their scientific dilemmas. However, this intensity was balanced by an almost poetic demeanor when discussing the implications of their work.

Oppenheimer's interactions with his team blended discussions with philosophical contemplations. He was known for encouraging his colleagues to think beyond conventions to question established norms and foster innovation. At the time, he provided guidance and clarity whenever they encountered confusion. His office at Los Alamos was always bustling with activity as scientists frequently dropped by for discussions and friendly chats. It was common to find Oppenheimer engrossed in a debate one moment and engaging in conversations about literature or Eastern philosophy the next.

His leadership was notable for his understanding of the aspect of the project. He acknowledged the pressure his team faced and made every effort to ensure their well-being. In addition to their pursuits, he organized gatherings, musical evenings, and philosophical discussions creating an environment where his team could find moments of relaxation and contemplation.

However, beneath this composed exterior, Oppenheimer grappled with the ethical implications of their creation. His reference to the Bhagavad Gita quote. "Now I am become Death, the destroyer of worlds." After the successful Trinity test provided a glimpse into the turmoil he experienced, it served as a reminder that while the Manhattan Project represented a scientific achievement, it also raised profound questions about humanity's responsibility and ethical boundaries in pursuit of knowledge.

Ultimately J. Robert Oppenheimer's leadership during the Manhattan Project showcased his ability to balance rigor with an understanding of emotions and ethical considerations.
He served as a guiding light leading his team through territories while also dealing with his inner struggles and contemplations.

The Weight of Creation: Ethical Dilemmas:

The explosion of the atomic bomb during the Trinity test in 1945 was not just a scientific victory; it was a moment that made many involved in the project contemplate deep ethical questions. As the blinding flash of the explosion illuminated the landscape of New Mexico, it became a catalyst for self-reflection. For individuals, the initial excitement and pride in their achievement quickly gave way to an overwhelming realization of the immense destructive power they had unleashed.

Among those grappling with this conflict, J. Robert Oppenheimer's response stands out as symbolic. Drawing inspiration from Hindu scripture, the Bhagavad Gita, he famously stated, "Now I become Death, the destroyer of worlds," capturing the nature of creation and destruction. This sentiment was not unique to Oppenheimer. Many scientists, engineers, and workers involved in the project experienced pride, guilt, and fear. They had accomplished what was once deemed impossible. But at what cost?

The subsequent bombings of Hiroshima and Nagasaki further intensified these dilemmas. The horrific images of devastation, harrowing survivor accounts, and sheer magnitude of suffering brought debates about atomic bomb morality into stark reality. Some scientists, including Leo Szilard, who initially supported the development of the bomb as a deterrent against Nazi Germany, later became critics of its use on civilian populations. On the hand, Edward Teller believed that the bombings were necessary to expedite the end of the war and ultimately save lives.

The ethical dilemmas surrounding these bombings extended beyond their aftermath. As the Cold War took hold and the arms race intensified, many individuals involved in the Manhattan Project were at the forefront of discussions about proliferation, arms control, and global security. The scientists responsible for ushering in the age now grappled with its implications for humanity's future.

For many of them, carrying the weight of their creation became a burden. They had unleashed something upon the world. Opening Pandora's box forever. Their internal struggles with grappling with implications serve as a reminder of how science, ethics, and human values intersect in complex ways. In records, the Manhattan Project showcases human innovation and profoundly contemplates bearing responsibility when wielding unprecedented power.

Life at Los Alamos: Beyond the Bomb:

Perched on the mesas of New Mexico, Los Alamos was a world of its own. The seclusion, both in terms of location and mindset, fostered an environment where the brightest minds of a generation not worked but also lived together. The secrecy surrounding the Manhattan Project meant that life at Los Alamos vastly differed from what people were accustomed to. Families were uprooted identities. A new way of life took shape.

Days at Los Alamos were intense, often starting before sunrise and stretching into the hours of the night. Laboratories buzzed with activity as equations filled chalkboards and passionate debates reverberated through the hallways. The urgency of the war and the immense responsibility they carried meant that work consumed their every moment. However, amidst this intensity, there was a realization that balance was necessary. Oppenheimer, being a leader, understood that for his team to succeed, they needed more than intellectual stimulation; they needed a sense of community and moments to recharge.

Evenings at Los Alamos presented a contrast to the demanding days. As twilight painted over the mesas, the community came alive in a way. Makeshift theaters showcased plays and movies while music filled the air with concerts and sing-alongs.

Despite their involvement in quantum mechanics, scientists at Los Alamos also found time for activities like playing tennis, teaching children, and participating in local dances. These ordinary pursuits played a role in boosting morale and fostering a sense of camaraderie among the scientific community.

Families and children brought a sense of normality to Los Alamos. Schools were. The sound of children's laughter became a backdrop. Completely oblivious to the work undertaken by their parents, they reveled in the open fields and found joy in forming lifelong friendships and creating cherished memories.

However, beneath this surface appearance of life lay reminders of the gravity of their project. Security checks, restricted areas, and the ubiquitous military personnel served as symbols highlighting the war and the crucial nature of their efforts. Even casual conversations were laced with caution since discussions about work were strictly off-limits.

The coexistence of groundbreaking endeavors with routines formed a captivating tapestry at Los Alamos. It was a place where Nobel laureates and young scientists dined together, where discussions about fission would seamlessly transition into debates about literature and philosophy.

The unique blend of intelligence, culture, and camaraderie at Los Alamos made it more than a facility. It embodied the best of humanity, where people joined forces to overcome obstacles.

When contemplating my time at Los Alamos, it becomes clear that although the atomic bomb was the result of the project, the real essence lay in the bonds formed between individuals, shared moments, and the unwavering determination of a united community.

The Unsung Heroes: Women of the Manhattan Project:

The Manhattan Projects narrative often focuses on its heroes. It's important to recognize the significant contributions made by women to understand the magnitude of this endeavor. Women played roles in this project ranging from scientific research to administrative support, and their stories bring a rich and multifaceted perspective to its history.

Leona Woods is a standout figure who exemplifies brilliance and determination. As one of the physicists involved in the project, Woods played a crucial role in constructing and operating the Chicago Pile 1, the world's first nuclear reactor. Her work wasn't simply about expertise. They also symbolized breaking barriers in a field dominated by men. Beyond her contributions to reactor construction, Woods's insights and expertise were highly valued as she closely collaborated with individuals like Enrico Fermi. Her involvement proved vital to ensuring the operation of the reactor.

Jean Tatlock may not have been directly engaged in aspects of the project; nevertheless, she had an impact on its most prominent figure – J. Robert Oppenheimer. As a psychiatrist by profession, Tatlock shared an emotional bond with Oppenheimer. Their relationship served as a platform for discussing literature, politics, and philosophy – providing Oppenheimer with both a sounding board and emotional support during the project's challenging phases.

Tatlock's influence went beyond providing support; her political beliefs and advocacy for peace and disarmament greatly influenced Oppenheimer's war position on nuclear weapons.

In addition to these individuals, the Manhattan Project involved the participation of women in various roles. One example is Charlotte Serber, a physicist who transitioned into the role of a librarian. She was entrusted with the responsibility of managing information for the project. Her contribution was important in ensuring scientists had access to information while maintaining project secrecy. Another group of women known as the "Calutron Girls" worked at Oak Ridge, operating calutrons used for uranium enrichment. Their work though they may not have fully grasped its significance at the time, played a role in the success of the project.

The women who participated in the Manhattan Project were not observers or mere supporters; they actively shaped events with their expertise, determination, and resilience. Their stories often take a backseat to those of their counterparts. Serve as a testament to the collaboration and innovation that defined this project. They remind us that groundbreaking endeavors are not limited to a few but are built upon the efforts of many individuals. Throughout history, as we delve into the story of the Manhattan Project, we must never forget and pay tribute to the overlooked heroes who made significant contributions.

The Aftermath: Living with the Legacy:

The explosion of the bombs over Hiroshima and Nagasaki marked the culmination of years of effort. However, for many involved in the Manhattan Project, it also signaled the beginning of a struggle with the ethical and societal consequences of their creation. The world had changed irreversibly. Those at the forefront of this transformation had a mix of emotions.

J. Robert Oppenheimer, the leader of the project, embodied this conflict. In the aftermath of the bombings, he felt remorse and famously quoted from the Bhagavad Gita; "Now I am become Death, the destroyer of worlds." This introspection led him to advocate for control over energy and end arms competition – perspectives that eventually clashed with political and military establishments.

Oppenheimer's journey was one among many. Scientists like Edward Teller called the "father of the hydrogen bomb," believed in developing weapons as a deterrent against potential adversaries. Teller's stance was rooted in an approach to politics during the Cold War era when maintaining a balance of power was seen as crucial for maintaining peace.

On the hand, numerous scientists who witnessed the destructive power of their creation emerged as strong advocates for disarmament. Influential figures like Leo Szilard and Linus Pauling actively promoted arms control measures emphasizing the threat posed by the spread of weapons. Their activism came at a professional cost shedding light on the broader societal debates of that era.

Beyond the realms of power and academia, the impact of the Manhattan Project resonated deeply with people. With its potential and dangers, the Atomic Age became a theme in literature, art, and popular culture. The dual nature of atoms –an energy source and a harbinger of destruction – captured the imagination.

For those involved in Los Alamos during those war years, it was a time for introspection and reassessment. Many returned to pursuits, while others pursued careers in industry or policymaking. However, the presence of the atomic bomb's shadow loomed large over their choices and personal philosophies. The connections forged during those years remained strong, with reunions and gatherings serving as opportunities for shared memories and contemplation.

In records, the Manhattan Project stands as evidence of resourcefulness and ambition. Its aftermath serves as a reminder of the responsibilities that accompany groundbreaking discoveries.

For those deeply involved in the project, the legacy encompassed a range of emotions and reflections—pride, regret, support, and self-reflection. Their unique and powerful experiences provide us with an understanding of the obstacles and ethical dilemmas encountered by trailblazers in the realm where science, ethics, and society converge.

Human Dimension of Scientific Endeavor

The Manhattan Project, often described in terms of its accomplishments and global ramifications, was fundamentally a human expedition. This chapter has unveiled the range of emotions, aspirations, dilemmas, and reflections that interwove the lives of those at the center of this undertaking.

J. Robert Oppenheimer, the leader, embodied intellectual brilliance and profound self-reflection. His interactions, leadership style, and eventual contemplation of the project embody the combination of pride in achievement and the weighty burden of ethical responsibility. However, beyond

Oppenheimer himself, a multitude of voices from Los Alamos. Including physicists and overlooked female contributors. Paint a vibrant picture of life in the shadow cast by creation. Their stories are filled with moments of joy, uncertainty, camaraderie, and introspection; together, they form a mosaic depicting experiences against the backdrop of one of history's significant scientific endeavors.

As we conclude this chapter, it becomes clear that the Manhattan Project encompassed more than the birth of an atomic bomb. It revolved around its participants. Their dreams and challenges were faced along their journey, as their victories were achieved. All intertwined with deep introspection. These stories serve as a reminder that behind every milestone lies human experiences, which are equally as momentous as the discoveries themselves.

CHAPTER 3: THE ETHICAL LABYRINTH.

J. Robert Oppenheimer is a historical figure who has sparked intrigue and debate. His contributions to science are undoubtedly significant. The challenges associated with his work have solidified his place in our collective memory. The era of power initiated by the explosion of the atomic bomb was a time of remarkable scientific advancement and deep moral contemplation. This juxtaposition had an impact on Oppenheimer personally.

The Weight of Creation:

The detonation of the bomb was not just a display of human ingenuity; it represented a moment that carried both creation and destruction in equal measure. When the mushroom cloud soared above the New Mexico desert during the Trinity test, it symbolized an era where humanity could harness the forces of the universe. This achievement is significant as it came with implications that would have long-lasting effects for future generations.

J. Robert Oppenheimer found himself at the center of this transformative change. His leadership in the Manhattan Project brought together some of the minds of the 20th century, all working toward a single daunting objective. However, as excitement over their accomplishment waned, Oppenheimer faced dilemmas associated with his work. The immense power demonstrated by bombs during their devastating trials served as a reminder of the responsibilities accompanying such knowledge. While some physicists hailed these bombs as crowning achievements for humanity, others—Oppenheimer included— questioned their implications. The bombings in Hiroshima and Nagasaki further intensified these reflections.

The immense devastation, the destruction of cities, and the tragic loss of innocent lives made the ethical dilemmas of the atomic age incredibly clear. When Oppenheimer quoted from the Bhagavad Gita saying, "Now I am become Death, the destroyer of worlds, " it wasn't an expression but an admission of the profound internal conflict he experienced. This mixture of pride, remorse, and self-reflection captured the nature of the age. Science had unlocked the mysteries of atoms. At what price?

Oppenheimer's personal journey symbolized soul-searching within the broader scientific community as humanity grappled with the implications of power. The atomic bomb, with its capability, raised questions that went beyond science itself. It delved into philosophy, ethics, and our very essence as beings. Was pursuing knowledge worth any consequences? Could science remain impartial in light of its creations? Did it carry a moral responsibility?

Oppenheimer's reflections on these matters were profound and often conflicting. He believed in science's potential for improving life and knew its possible dangers. The atomic bomb, in his perspective, symbolized this nature. It showcased the abilities of humanity while also serving as a constant reminder of the moral responsibilities accompanying such brilliance.

When we look back at history, the era of power will not be recognized for its scientific achievements but also for the profound ethical dilemmas it presented. At the core of this era were individuals like Oppenheimer, who found themselves grappling with questions about creation and destruction in their pursuit of knowledge.

Post-War Ethical Debates:

The end of World War II didn't resolve the ethical dilemmas brought forth by the atomic age. Instead, the period after the war became a testing ground for discussing the ethical aspects of nuclear power and weapons. The world had witnessed the capacity of atomic energy, and the initial triumph was soon overshadowed by deep introspection among scientists, policymakers, and the general public.

J. Robert Oppenheimer found himself at the center of these debates due to his role in developing the bomb. His position was unique as he was both a figure in shaping the age and one of its most vocal critics. The bombings of Hiroshima and Nagasaki left a lasting impact on him, prompting him to question his work and the wider implications of scientific advancements. Oppenheimer saw beyond applications; for him, the atomic bomb symbolized humanity's ability to harness immense power and an enormous responsibility to use it wisely. The geopolitical landscape during the war era further complicated these ethical considerations.

The Cold War was on the horizon, and the United States and the Soviet Union, once allies, found themselves in a military standoff. The competition for dominance became an aspect of this rivalry. As countries stockpiled weapons, there was a looming threat of destruction. Oppenheimer, being practical-minded, recognized the dangers of this arms race. He advocated for oversight of energy, believing that working together could help reduce the risks associated with uncontrolled nuclear proliferation.

However, not everyone agreed with Oppenheimer's views. Many influential figures saw his stance as naive and potentially harmful to security. They argued that given the threat from the Soviet Union, the United States needed to maintain its advantage in capabilities. This difference in perspectives highlighted a conflict during the age, finding a balance between national security needs and ethical responsibility.

The community had debates about their role in this new world order. The Manhattan Project demonstrated how scientists could profoundly impact geopolitics. However, this influence raised questions about boundaries in exploration. Should scientists pursue knowledge without considering its applications? Did they have an obligation to consider the broader societal consequences of their work?

These were not just questions. They had real-world consequences for research, funding, and global cooperation.

To summarize, the ethical discussions after the war about energy were complex; they covered a wide range of topics, including geopolitical strategy and the moral obligations of scientists. For individuals like Oppenheimer, these debates held significance as they reflected the relationship between science, ethics, and politics in the era of atomic technology.

Science at the Crossroads:

The 20th century posed a challenge for humanity due to the progress in scientific discoveries. On the one hand, it brought excitement and breakthroughs uncovering nature's secrets and pushing boundaries. On the hand, it also made us aware of the implications that accompanied these advancements. This paradox was particularly evident in the field of research, where there was a balance between groundbreaking innovation and potential devastation.

J. Robert Oppenheimer experienced this tension on a level. As a physicist, he was deeply familiar with the allure of exploring the unknown and the thrill of making discoveries. The world of quantum mechanics, with its particles and waves, offered fascination for his curious mind. However, it also led to the creation of humanity's weapon. This contrast between exploration and its potential for harm became a recurring theme throughout Oppenheimer's life.

The wider scientific community also faced a moment during this era—the advent of the age introduced numerous profound questions. Were there areas of knowledge that were better left unexplored? Were any discoveries so powerful and dangerous that it was better for them to remain a mystery? These were not just thoughts; they had real-world consequences. The pursuit of knowledge, once considered an endeavor, was now being scrutinized.

Oppenheimer, known for his leanings, often pondered these questions. He believed that the essence of science lay in the quest for understanding. It was about unraveling the enigmas of the universe one equation at a time. However, he also recognized the weight of responsibility that accompanied understanding.

This period of introspection and debate extended beyond the community. Society as a whole grappled with the implications brought by the age. Culture, politics, and philosophy transformed due to groundbreaking discoveries. Science fiction surged in popularity from being a niche genre to reflecting society's aspirations and anxieties about what lay. Philosophers engaged in discussions regarding science's role in society while policymakers struggled to keep up with technological advancements.

Oppenheimer's voice emerged during this era as one advocating reason and introspection. He advocated for a rounded approach to investigation, one that considered ethical considerations. According to him, pursuing knowledge wasn't merely an end in itself but rather a path toward understanding the universe and our place within it. However, he also believed that this understanding came with a responsibility to utilize it wisely, ensuring that the outcomes of endeavors benefited everyone without causing harm.

In essence, during Oppenheimer's era, the intersection where science stood wasn't about research or ethics alone. It represented something profound—the very essence of knowledge, its purpose, and its implications. It served as a reflection of humanity's struggles to reconcile its curiosity with the moral obligations inherent in our existence.

The AEC Hearing: A Collision of Ethics and Politics:

The 1954 hearing conducted by the Atomic Energy Commission (AEC) and its subsequent revocation of J. Robert Oppenheimer's security clearance remains an event in the history of science. While it may seem like a matter on the surface, the hearing delves into a complex web of ethical dilemmas, political maneuverings, and personal disputes.

Having already established himself as the leader of the Manhattan Project, Oppenheimer had secured his place in history. However, as the post-war era unfolded and the Cold War took hold, his stance on proliferation diverged from mainstream opinions. His vocal reservations about developing hydrogen bombs and his support for the control of energy were viewed by many politicians and military figures as naive or even disloyal. These views were deeply rooted in his beliefs regarding the dangers posed by a nuclear arms race leading to direct conflicts with influential individuals within the U.S. Government.

The hearing itself was quite dramatic. It spanned weeks during which various witnesses— scientists and military officials—were summoned to provide testimony.
Oppenheimer's previous affiliations during his time at Berkeley came under scrutiny. He faced accusations of sympathizing with communism primarily due to his associations and opposition to nuclear weapons programs. The proceedings were filled with

drama and became more than a trial of Oppenheimer's character; they also questioned his loyalty.

However, beyond the details of the hearing, broader questions arose regarding the role of scientists in the age. Could scientists, with their understanding of the consequences of their work, remain politically neutral? Was there space for dissenting voices, especially when they challenged prevailing military doctrines? The AEC hearing served as a reflection of these debates. It highlighted the relationship between science and politics, ethics, and national security.

Ultimately Oppenheimer's security clearance was revoked—a decision that effectively ended his impact on U.S. Policy. Nonetheless, the implications of the AEC hearing went beyond its aftermath. It emerged as a tale about the dangers of voicing dissent during a period overshadowed by paranoia. It underscored the challenges faced by scientists who knew how their creations could bring consequences and sought to shape policies based on ethical considerations.

The AEC hearing didn't solely revolve around J. Robert Oppenheimer. It served as a reflection of the tensions during that period encapsulating the essence of an era where the potential of energy clashed with genuine concerns about nuclear destruction. It serves as a reminder of the interplay between science, ethics, and politics in our contemporary world.

Navigating the Labyrinth:

The life of J. Robert Oppenheimer was a blend of brilliance intertwined with deep moral reflections. Being the mastermind behind the creation of the bomb, he found himself at crossroads where remarkable scientific achievement intersected with profound ethical dilemmas. The atomic age, with its potential for energy and unimaginable destruction, perfectly embodied the nature of scientific progress. With each significant breakthrough came important ethical considerations that demanded attention. Oppenheimer found himself in these thought-provoking discussions.

His journey mirrored the path of science throughout the century, from esteemed academic institutions to secretive laboratories in Los Alamos. The pursuit of knowledge, once regarded as a pursuit in its right, now carried far-reaching implications beyond the confines of laboratories. The atomic bomb, as both an instrument of war and diplomacy, became a symbol representing scientists' power and responsibility. Oppenheimer's introspection following Hiroshima and Nagasaki portrayed the soul-searching experienced by many within his field. Science has allowed humanity to harness energy; however, society had to navigate its usage guided by ethical considerations. However, Oppenheimer's story is not solely focused on dilemmas.

It is also a testament to the strength of the spirit. Despite the difficulties and controversies that defined his career, he consistently advocated for the utilization of knowledge. In his years, he supported nuclear disarmament and envisioned a world driven by international cooperation, demonstrating his belief in a brighter and more enlightened future.

When we retrace Oppenheimer's path through the complexities of his time, we are reminded that the questions he grappled with have lasting relevance. The delicate balance between progress and accountability, innovation and introspection remains as important today as it was during Oppenheimer's era. Oppenheimer's legacy serves as a guiding light urging us to approach the future with ambition while upholding strong ethical values as we find ourselves on the verge of frontiers- from artificial intelligence to genetic engineering.

PHILOSOPHICAL INTERLUDES AND DEBATES:

J. Robert Oppenheimer's life was not defined by his accomplishments but also by his deep reflections on philosophy. As the leader of the Manhattan Project, he played a role in one of the significant scientific endeavors of the 20th century. However, when the atomic bomb was detonated, it ushered in an era—that presented Oppenheimer with complex ethical and philosophical challenges.

The atomic bomb, while an impressive display of engineering expertise, brought forth a multitude of dilemmas. The immense destructive power it possessed, capable of obliterating cities and reshaping the course of conflicts, raised questions beyond scientific inquiry. Oppenheimer, profoundly influenced by Western philosophies, grappled with these questions by turning to ancient texts and philosophical writings for guidance.

The Weight of Creation:

The bomb explosion was a moment for J. Robert Oppenheimer, filled with conflicting emotions. On the one hand, it symbolized the advancements in science and the relentless pursuit of knowledge achieved through years of research and collaboration. Oppenheimer, leading the Manhattan Project, successfully harnessed the forces of the universe, unlocking unimaginable power. The brilliance of the scientists involved in their innovative theories and engineering breakthroughs and their ability to overcome challenges make this achievement unmatched in history.

However, this extraordinary accomplishment also carried a burden. The bomb's immense power brought forth moral implications that would have long-lasting consequences.

Oppenheimer, well-versed in literature and philosophy, found himself grappling with the magnitude of their creation. After witnessing the aftermath of Trinity's tests, he recited a line from the Bhagavad Gita; "Now I am become Death, the destroyer of worlds." This profound statement reflected his struggle as he tried to reconcile their marvel with its potential for devastating destruction.

The Bhagavad Gita is a scripture that explores topics such as duty, righteousness, and wars' moral complexities—themes that deeply resonated with Oppenheimer's turmoil in light of what they had accomplished scientifically.

The experience of having emotions was not unique to Oppenheimer. Many scientists who were part of the project also felt pride and apprehension. However, as the leader, Oppenheimer bore a burden. He had gathered the resources, guided his team, and made decisions that led to that momentous event. Now he confronted the reality that their creation could profoundly alter history for better or worse.

In the following years, Oppenheimer's contemplation on ethical matters deepened. The atomic bomb became a symbol for him— a representation of how scientific discoveries possess both the potential to uplift humanity and the power to bring about its downfall. This period of introspection marked the beginning of Oppenheimer's exploration into the challenges brought forth by the atomic age—a journey during which he advocated for control, diplomacy, and responsible usage of atomic energy.

"The Weight of Creation" transcended weapon development; it marked the dawn of an era—the age—an era that raised profound questions about scientific responsibility itself, ethical dilemmas surrounding discoveries, and scientists' role in shaping humanity's destiny.

Hiroshima, Nagasaki, and the Moral Quandary:

The bombings of Hiroshima and Nagasaki in August 1945 are considered two of the moments in recent history. These events, being the instances when nuclear weapons were used in warfare, brought World War II to an end. However, the immediate military success was overshadowed by the suffering caused and the moral questions it raised.

For Oppenheimer witnessing the devastating power of bombs was both an achievement and an ethical dilemma. The haunting images of mushroom clouds over Hiroshima and Nagasaki represented the nature of progress, our ability to make groundbreaking advancements alongside the potential for catastrophic destruction. In the aftermath, entire cities were reduced to rubble tens of thousands lost their lives instantly. Countless others suffered from the long-term effects of radiation exposure. These distressing scenes prompted discussions about discoveries, responsibilities, and consequences.

Oppenheimer personally struggled with conflicting emotions regarding these bombings. While he understood the reasoning behind deploying bombs, he was deeply troubled by the loss of civilian lives. His internal conflict mirrored debates on whether using such weapons against civilian populations was ethically justifiable.

Was the war's conclusion potentially saving many lives by avoiding a prolonged conflict a valid justification for the immediate devastation and long-lasting suffering inflicted upon Hiroshima and Nagasaki?

In the aftermath of the bombings, Oppenheimer emerged as a proponent of disarmament and international regulation of atomic energy. He firmly believed that the global community needed to unite to ensure that the horrors witnessed in Hiroshima and

Nagasaki would never be repeated. However, his stance often clashed with military establishments that viewed weapons as indispensable tools for deterrence during the emerging Cold War era.

The bombings also sparked ethical debates that transcended boundaries. Scholars in philosophy, theology, and ethics grappled with questions regarding the morality of employing weapons of destruction, the essence of warfare, and scientists' responsibilities in the world. Oppenheimer's unique position at the crossroads of science and ethics made him a central figure in these discussions. His contemplations on Hiroshima and Nagasaki, influenced by Western traditions, contributed depth and complexity to ongoing dialogues.

The bombings of Hiroshima and Nagasaki represented profound moral turning points. For J. Robert Oppenheimer and the world, these events indicated the moral challenges that come with scientific and technological progress.

Harnessing Atomic Energy: Promise and Peril:

The beginning of the era not brought the ominous presence of mushroom clouds but also sparked hope for a new energy source that could transform the world. With its potential, Atomic energy offered a solution to our hunger for power and progress. The allure of power was captivating; it could provide electricity to cities, fuel industries, and potentially revolutionize societies. The dream of a world with affordable electricity, where blackouts were a thing of the past and energy crises were no longer a concern, seemed within reach.

However, this promise came with its share of challenges. The same process that fueled the sun and destructive atomic bombs could be harnessed for purposes. It required careful handling and management. The reactors needed to tap into this power were machines. While uranium fuel was plentiful, it presented its difficulties. Issues such as uranium mining, enrichment processes, and safe waste disposal became concerns.

There was always the looming possibility of accidents. Although the technology behind power was advanced, it was not flawless. The world was harshly reminded of this reality through incidents like the Three Mile Island accident in the United States and the Chornobyl disaster in the Soviet Union. These events highlighted the risks associated with power, raising concerns about safety measures, regulatory oversight, and the long-term consequences of nuclear accidents on human health and the environment.

Oppenheimer understood both the benefits and challenges of atomic energy. He supported power for its purposes but also recognized its difficulties. He advocated for collaboration in energy, believing that its advantages should be shared globally while maintaining strict safeguards. His vision encompassed nations working together to engage in research exchange practices and address issues related to waste disposal, safety protocols, and proliferation concerns.

However, the issue of nuclear weapons proliferation added a layer of complexity to discussions. The same technology that could provide electricity to cities also had the potential to be a weapon of destruction. The boundary between applications and military use was delicate, deeply troubling Oppenheimer as he feared a nuclear arms race amidst an already tense Cold War era.

Ultimately the exploration of energy was a captivating journey filled with contradictions. It offered hope for a more prosperous future. It also brought forth significant obstacles that demanded careful handling. Oppenheimer's thoughts and viewpoints give us a glimpse into the nature of an era where humanity found itself at the threshold of an era delicately balancing the potential for advancement against the dangers of unparalleled power.

Dialogues with Contemporary Thinkers:

Amidst the whirlwind of ethical challenges during the era, J. Robert Oppenheimer found solace and inspiration through deep conversations with some of the brilliant thinkers of his time— these interactions, intense and introspective, offered perspectives that profoundly impacted Oppenheimer's worldview.

One noteworthy connection was with Albert Einstein. Despite being notable figures in physics, they held differing views on the bomb and its consequences. Einstein, who initially supported its development by signing a letter to President Roosevelt, later expressed remorse, saying, "If I had known that the Germans would fail to create a bomb, I would have refrained from taking any action." Oppenheimer engaged in discussions with Einstein regarding the obligations of scientists, particularly about weapons capable of mass destruction. These dialogues were characterized by respect and served as a reminder of the complex nature of scientific progress and its potential implications for humanity.

Jean Paul Sartre, one of the voices in existentialist philosophy at that time, also played a significant role in shaping Oppenheimer's philosophical journey. Sartre's exploration of freedom, responsibility, and existential angst deeply resonated with Oppenheimer's internal struggles.

Their conversations delved into the essence of existence, the weight of decision-making, and the existential crisis triggered by the age. Sartre's viewpoint, grounded in the belief that humans are destined to be free and must shoulder the consequences of their choices, gave Oppenheimer a framework to grapple with the dilemmas he encountered.

In addition, to engaging with Einstein and Sartre, Oppenheimer engaged in discussions with a range of intellectuals spanning poets, philosophers, historians, and political thinkers. These exchanges often occurred informally at conferences, personal meetings, or social gatherings – a testament to Oppenheimer's thirst for knowledge. They allowed him to widen his perspective on the challenges of his time by placing advancements within a cultural, philosophical, and ethical context.

In essence, these dialogues were more than exercises for Oppenheimer; they served as a lifeline – guiding him through the turbulent waters of the atomic age. They offered insights into his work while posing thought-provoking questions and creating an environment for introspection and contemplation. Through these interactions, Oppenheimer sought not to grasp the implications of his research but also to strike a balance between scientific discoveries' allure and their accompanying ethical responsibilities.

The Cold War and the Hydrogen Bomb Dilemma:

The era known as the Cold War was much more than a standoff between the Soviet Union and the United States. It was a time marked by an arms race, ideological clashes, and the constant fear of catastrophe. People worldwide held their breath as these two superpowers, armed with weapons, carefully balanced their strength. In this context, the development of the hydrogen bomb, also known as the thermonuclear bomb, became a point of contention.

The hydrogen bomb represented an escalation in comparison to the bombs that were dropped on Hiroshima and Nagasaki. Its creation posed not challenges but also profound ethical and philosophical dilemmas. Its sheer destructive power raised questions about the boundaries of exploration and the moral responsibilities of those involved in such groundbreaking discoveries.

J. Robert Oppenheimer, who had witnessed firsthand the effects of bombs, found himself torn about pursuing the development of a hydrogen bomb. While he acknowledged arguments supporting its creation in response to nuclear advancements, he could not ignore its moral implications. The potential for such a weapon to cause destruction and loss of life weighed heavily on his conscience. Oppenheimer's concerns regarding the hydrogen bomb were not just personal; they stemmed from a philosophical perspective on the role of science in society. He believed that scientists, as creators and innovators, held a responsibility to contemplate the implications of their work. According to Oppenheimer, the development of the hydrogen bomb was not solely an undertaking; it also reflected humanity's choices and values.

These convictions often led Oppenheimer into conflicts with military establishments. Advocates for the hydrogen bomb saw it as a deterrent against Soviet aggression. They argued that in the high-stakes realm of Cold War politics, demonstrating strength and maintaining superiority were crucial. However, Oppenheimer viewed the bomb as a menace—a weapon for initiating an era marred by an unparalleled global catastrophe.

The debates surrounding the hydrogen bomb extended beyond strategy and geopolitics. They delved into inquiries about discoveries of nature, human ambitions, limits, and ethical considerations associated with wielding immense power. Oppenheimer's standpoint, although controversial, at that time serves as a reminder of the challenges and dilemmas faced by scientists and intellectuals in an era of technological advancements and complex geopolitical dynamics.

Looking back, the dilemma of the hydrogen bomb truly represents the core of the Cold War era. It was a time characterized by advancements, ideological conflicts, and the constant fear of nuclear destruction. By examining

Oppenheimer's experiences, we can understand how science, ethics, and global politics intertwined during that period.

Navigating the Ethical Maze:

J. Robert Oppenheimer's life exemplified the balance between groundbreaking accomplishments and the ethical dilemmas often accompanying such progress. As the "Father of the Atomic Bomb," he was aware of the Pandora's box opened by the emergence of nuclear weapons. The immense destructive power unleashed by these bombs was not an impressive technological feat but also a stark reminder of the responsibilities associated with wielding such immense power.

The mid-20th century was a time of change and uncertainty. The horrors endured during World War II deeply affected people worldwide. The advent of technology added further complexity to an already intricate global landscape. In this context, Oppenheimer found himself at the center of discussions that extended beyond science and delved into areas such as philosophy, ethics, and politics. His firm belief in using science for humanity's betterment often clashed with the realities of the age. The bombings in Hiroshima and Nagasaki, while instrumental in bringing an end to war, also emphasized the implications of employing such devastating weapons against civilian populations.

Oppenheimer's philosophical perspective, shaped by both Western ideologies, provided him with a framework through which he contemplated these challenges.

His reflections extended beyond the aftermath of the bombings. As the world moved into the era of the Cold War with its arms race and the looming threat of destruction, it raised more profound questions about scientists' responsibility in shaping humanity's future. Oppenheimer's support for the control of energy and his concerns about developing the hydrogen bomb reflected his deep belief in the necessity of ethical considerations guiding scientific endeavors.

However, this journey was not without its difficulties. Though driven by a concern for humanity's well-being, Oppenheimer's views often clashed with military establishments. The revocation of his security clearance in the 1950s served as a reminder of the turbulent relationship between science, ethics, and politics. Nevertheless, despite facing adversity, Oppenheimer remained unwavering in his convictions. He became an inspiration for generations of scientists and thinkers.

Looking back, J. Robert Oppenheimer's navigation through the complexities of the age serves as a poignant reminder of how intricate human progress can be. His story highlights the importance of self-reflection, dialogue, and ethical considerations in shaping advancements.

As we find ourselves on the brink of horizons in the realms of science and technology, Oppenheimer's legacy provides us wisdom regarding the obstacles and obligations that accompany our pursuit of knowledge.

CHAPTER 4: ESPIONAGE AND THE SHADOWS OF THE COLD WAR.

The mid-20th century was an period in human history. After World War II, countries found themselves engaged in a kind of warfare that didn't rely on battlefields or open combat. This era was known as the Cold War, a prolonged and often secretive struggle for supremacy between two superpowers of that time; the United States and the Soviet Union. The atomic bomb played a role in this chess match, ending the previous war and setting the stage for what was to come.

The bombings of Hiroshima and Nagasaki in 1945 demonstrated the power of weapons. These events marked the end of World War II and also signaled the beginning of a new age defined by nuclear capabilities. The world had witnessed firsthand what atomic energy could do, sparking a race among nations to harness, control, and potentially weaponize this power. As countries rushed to build their arsenals, it became clear that dominance in this atomic era equated to global superiority.

However, the Cold War extended beyond weapon stockpiling; it was ultimately a clash of ideologies – capitalism versus communism, democracy versus totalitarianism. Every action taken and decision made during this period was analyzed within the context of this conflict.

In this high-stakes game, gathering information was as crucial as any explosive or bullet. Espionage, the art of obtaining information, became a tactic for both superpowers. Spies, double agents, and informants created a network of intrigue worldwide, with each side striving to gain a hand over the other.

J. Robert Oppenheimer playing a role in developing the bomb, found himself at the center of this whirlwind of political maneuvering and undercover operations. His brilliance as a physicist was undeniable. In the realm of the Cold War, brilliance alone wasn't sufficient. Loyalties were questioned, and distinguishing between friend and foe often became blurry. As we delve into this chapter, we'll explore Oppenheimer's life during this era—a life intertwined with espionage and politics—revealing the challenges and dilemmas faced by those standing at the crossroads of advancements and global affairs.

The Atomic Age and the Rise of Espionage:

The beginning of the Atomic Age marked a change in the world's landscape. When the atomic bomb was successfully detonated in 1945, humanity gained access to a power that was once exclusive to nature. The atomic bomb, with its capabilities, became a symbol of dominance and an invaluable bargaining tool that nations sought to possess.

While the United States celebrated its newfound power, it quickly became apparent that this advantage wouldn't last forever. The Soviet Union recognized the importance of weapons and was determined to bridge the technological gap. This race for supremacy wasn't confined to laboratories and reactors; it extended into information gathering. Espionage, an aged practice in statecraft, took on renewed significance. Intelligence agencies on both sides of the Iron Curtain intensified their operations, aiming to gather every bit of information about their adversary's capabilities.

The stakes were incredibly high as espionage had the potential to shift the balance of power dramatically, giving one side an advantage. This sense of urgency led to a proliferation of operations with spies infiltrating research facilities, diplomatic missions, and even academic institutions.

The world of intelligence, once confined to locations and clandestine meetings, had now made its way into the realm of science.

However, during the Atomic Age, espionage was not solely reliant on agents. Technological advancements played a role in this domain. Wiretapping, surveillance devices, and early forms of espionage became tools in this high-stakes game. Every conversation, correspondence, or research paper could yield information.

Despite its sophistication, espionage was tinged with desperation and paranoia during this era. The looming threat of destruction was palpable. Both superpowers were acutely aware that a single piece of information falling into the hands could result in catastrophe. This fear often bordered on obsession. It led to some of history's audacious and daring intelligence operations.

Looking back, the rise of espionage during the Atomic Age seems like a consequence of the circumstances. In a world teetering on the edge of war, knowledge became power. Recognizing this fact, nations went to lengths to safeguard their secrets while uncovering those held by their adversaries.

The Scientific Community Under Scrutiny:

The advent of the era not brought remarkable scientific advancements but also created a climate of intense scrutiny and suspicion. As countries grappled with the implications of power, the scientific community found itself at the heart of this global order. Atomic research became a security matter with its potential for both destructive applications. Consequently, scientists who previously pursued knowledge within the safety of their laboratories were now thrust into the spotlight, their work subjected to oversight and occasionally met with suspicion.

This newfound attention had both negative consequences. On the one hand, the significance of their works was acknowledged, leading to increased funding opportunities, cutting-edge facilities, and chances for collaboration. On the other hand, it challenged the essence of scientific inquiry that thrives on open exchange and collaboration. The free flow of ideas—fundamental to research pursuits—was hindered by the necessity for secrecy and compartmentalization. Researchers had to exercise caution as they knew their domestic and international communications were likely being monitored. The charged atmosphere was further compounded by concerns about espionage and perceived threats.

The news that the Soviet Union had successfully tested a bomb in 1949 earlier than expected by the Western world caused a great deal of shock and concern within the intelligence and scientific communities of the United States. It led to accusations and investigations resulting in loyalty pledges and background checks for research participants. The case of the Rosenbergs though not directly connected to the core community, had an effect. It highlighted the possibility that secrets could be leaked to powers breaching the integrity of the research community.

This was a time of reflection for J. Robert Oppenheimer and his colleagues. They had to reconcile their dedication to inquiry with the realities of a world filled with geopolitical tensions. The ethical implications of their work on the destructive power of atomic bombs added another layer of complexity. Many individuals, including Oppenheimer himself, wrestled with dilemmas arising from their contributions leading to private debates about what path should be taken.

In essence, during the Cold War era, the scientific community found itself navigating territory. The pursuit of knowledge, for its sake, was juxtaposed against the realities of global politics and espionage.

It was a time that put researchers to the test, pushing them to find a harmony, between their love, for exploration and the demands of security.

Oppenheimer: A Figure of Interest:

Julius Robert Oppenheimer's significance in the field of research was undeniable. As the director of the Manhattan Project, he played a role in developing the world's first atomic bomb, which had profound and far-reaching impacts on global geopolitics. However, with great prominence came scrutiny as various national and international entities closely monitored Oppenheimer.

The controversies surrounding his life and affiliations became a subject of debate. Oppenheimer associated with individuals and groups who held leaning ideologies during his youth. While such associations were common among intellectuals during that era, they took on a tone amidst the charged atmosphere of the Cold War. His relationships, both past and present, were thoroughly examined through a lens of suspicion. His close ties to the Communist Party through his wife, brother, and many friends only fueled these concerns.

The Federal Bureau of Investigation (FBI), led by J. Edgar Hoover, took an interest in monitoring Oppenheimer's activities. Known for his seated mistrust of communists and his aggressive approach Hoover ensured that Oppenheimer was under surveillance.

The FBI gathered a file on him, keeping tabs on his movements monitoring his conversations, and even interviewing people he knew while pretending it was routine. This surveillance wasn't limited to activities within the country; the FBI was particularly interested in Oppenheimer's interactions with scientists from Eastern bloc countries.

However, it wasn't just Oppenheimer's past that attracted attention; it was also his viewpoints. Oppenheimer became more vocal about the ethical implications of weapons as the Cold War progressed. Many viewed his support for energy control and reservations about developing the hydrogen bomb as conflicting with national interests. Although these perspectives were rooted in understanding warfare's consequences, they often clashed with the more aggressive stance held by political and military leaders.

Oppenheimer's associations and outspoken opinions created a blend that led many to question where his loyalties truly lay. Was he genuinely dedicated to serving the United States and its interests? Did he align himself with causes? These simple questions were intricately entangled in a web of politics, ethics, and personal beliefs. Oppenheimer personified the intricacies of an era where the boundaries between science and politics were frequently indistinct, and loyalties were perpetually subject to scrutiny.

The AEC Hearing: A Defining Moment:

The 1954 Atomic Energy Commission (AEC) hearing was much more than an investigation. It marked a moment in scientific and political history during the tense Cold War era characterized by suspicion and fear. The hearing became a spectacle that exposed the interplay between science, ethics, and national security.

J. Robert Oppenheimer, renowned as the "Father of the Atomic Bomb, " was the center of this event. The hearing aimed to determine whether Oppenheimer's security clearance should be revoked, which was essential for him to continue his involvement in research. A wide range of charges were brought against him, including associations with those to communism and alleged inconsistencies in his testimonies regarding interactions with fellow scientists. However, beneath these formal accusations lurked concerns about Oppenheimer's stance on policy, particularly his outspoken opposition to developing an even more powerful weapon than an atomic bomb – the hydrogen bomb.

The proceedings were highly filled with intensity. Accompanied by his team, Oppenheimer faced a panel of interrogators who questioned him extensively on topics. Witnesses, both in support of and against him, were called upon to provide testimony presenting a portrait of a man who possessed brilliance and mystery. Their testimonies reveal the facts surrounding the case. It also sheds light on the ideological clashes at play. Oppenheimer's belief in oversight of energy clashed with the more aggressive stance held by many within the political and military establishment resulting in profound disagreements.

One poignant moment occurred during the hearing when Oppenheimer himself took the stand. He spoke candidly with emotion, reflecting on his journey from the ambitious days of the Manhattan Project to grappling with moral dilemmas in the atomic age. While he acknowledged his associations, he also emphasized his unwavering dedication to his country's security. His words underscored the challenges faced by scientists during an era when their discoveries carried ethical consequences.

The outcome of this hearing—the revocation of Oppenheimer's security clearance—had reaching implications for the community. It signaled a shift in the relationship between scientists and governmental authorities, placing loyalty and ideological conformity above all else. The decision evoked shock, outrage and resignation among individuals who saw it as a tale about expressing dissent within a deeply divided world. Looking back, the AEC hearing wasn't solely focused on Oppenheimer's security clearance. It served as a mirror of the era highlighting the difficulties of balancing exploration, ethical obligations, and national security in a world teetering on the edge of devastation.

The Interplay of Science and Politics:

The era of the Cold War, characterized by tensions and ideological conflicts, brought to light the complex relationship between science and politics. This period emphasized that scientific progress in physics went beyond mere scholarly pursuits confined within laboratories; it had implications for security, diplomacy, and the delicate balance of power.

An example of this intersection is J. Robert Oppenheimer's journey. As a scientist, he was motivated by a thirst for knowledge and an eagerness to unravel the mysteries of the universe. However, his groundbreaking contributions to atomic bomb research propelled him into the spotlight, making him a central figure in America's considerations. His involvement in the Manhattan Project showcased his brilliance. It highlighted ethical dilemmas associated with such discoveries—the ability to harness energy presented both power possibilities and grave threats of unprecedented devastation.

During that period, there was an atmosphere filled with suspicion and paranoia within the landscape. The nuclear arms race between superpowers resulted in scientists becoming entangled in espionage or counter-espionage activities. The nature of their work meant they were at risk of being targeted by intelligence agencies as it required collaboration and exchanging ideas across borders. Oppenheimer's own experiences, including the scrutiny he faced and the dramatic AEC hearing, mirrored the challenges faced by the community. They were questioned about their loyalties, had their intentions dissected, and often saw their work through a lens.

Reflecting on this era, it becomes clear that there is often a line between science and politics. Scientific discoveries with societal implications cannot be separated from their political contexts.

They are both influenced by. Have an impact on the geopolitical considerations of their time. For scientists like Oppenheimer, this dynamic raised questions about the role and responsibilities of the community. It compelled them to contemplate the consequences of their work and grapple with ethical considerations that arise when wielding such power.

As we look back on J. Robert Oppenheimer's life and legacy, his story serves as a reminder of the intricacies and difficulties faced by those who navigate the intersection of science and politics. It highlights the importance of a nuanced understanding of advancements while acknowledging their potential for progress and peril.

REAL-LIFE SPY STORIES AND INTRIGUES:

The Cold War, which occurred during the middle of the century, was marked by increased tensions, political maneuvers, and secret operations. The competition for dominance between the United States and the Soviet Union was not a matter of scientific progress but also involved intelligence activities and espionage. The realm of research, with its implications for global power dynamics, became a breeding ground for spies, double agents, and complex schemes. At the heart of this situation stood J. Robert Oppenheimer, a physicist whose contributions had already altered the course of history.

The Rosenberg Affair: A Tale of Atomic Espionage:

Few cases in Cold War espionage have captured public fascination, like the Rosenberg Affair. Julius and Ethel Rosenberg, an American couple, found themselves at the center of a whirlwind of controversy, intrigue, and fear that would forever define the early years of the atomic era.

Both Julius and Ethel were members of the Communist Party. Deeply involved in activism during the 1930s and 1940s. While their beliefs were not uncommon for that period, they would later become targets in a climate of suspicion following World War II. The United States celebrated its triumphs with the Manhattan Project and the end of WWII. This joy was short-lived. The shocking realization that America's wartime ally, the Soviet Union, had rapidly developed capabilities sent shockwaves through intelligence circles. The burning question on everyone's mind was simple; How did the Soviets manage to catch up?

This question triggered a hunt for leaks within America's atomic research community. Enough Julius Rosenberg, an engineer with connections to projects, became tangled in suspicions. Investigations revealed allegations that Julius had shared information about bombs with Soviet contacts through his network.

The evidence, though not direct, was incredibly incriminating. Recorded phone conversations, secret meetings, and testimonies from others accused of spying all pointed to Julius being a member of a spy network.

However, the arrest and subsequent trial of Juliuss' wife, Ethel Rosenberg, added a layer of drama and emotion to the case. She was accused of assisting her husband in his espionage activities by typing up the stolen atomic secrets that he then passed on to their Soviet contacts. The trial took place in 1951 and attracted media attention. Journalists from over the world crowded into the courtroom, eagerly absorbing every word and revelation. Throughout it all, Julius and Ethel steadfastly maintained their innocence, asserting they were victims of a hunt.

When the verdict was finally delivered, it arrived swiftly and without doubt; Julius and Ethel were found guilty of espionage with a sentence of death. Appeals for mercy poured in from sources within the country well as internationally. Influential figures such as the Pope and renowned physicist Albert Einstein pleaded for their lives to be spared. Unfortunately, given the prevailing atmosphere dominated by McCarthyism and fears surrounding infiltration ("Red Scare"), these pleas went unheard.

On the 19th of June in 1953, Julius and Ethel Rosenberg faced the punishment of leaving behind their two sons.

To this day, the Rosenberg Affair sparks debates and speculation. Was their guilt genuine? Were they merely made into scapegoats during a time of paranoia? While subsequent revelations, including decrypted communications, suggest that Julius was indeed involved in espionage activities, the degree of Ethel's involvement remains uncertain. Their trial and execution serve as a reminder of the tolls of espionage, the delicate nature of justice, and how global politics can profoundly impact individual lives.

Klaus Fuchs: The Insider's Betrayal:

Klaus Fuchs, a physicist from Germany, remains a figure in the history of atomic espionage. His journey from being a fascist activist in Germany to becoming a significant contributor to the Manhattan Project in the United States and eventually confessing to spying for the Soviet Union is a complex story filled with ideological conflicts, personal dilemmas, and the overarching influence of the Cold War.

Born in 1911, Fuchs witnessed the events that defined 20th-century Europe. He strongly opposed the rise of Nazism during his years in Germany. In response to this opposition, he joined the German Communist Party—a decision that would later have implications for him. Escaping from Nazi rule, Fuchs sought safety in Britain, where his expertise in physics led him to become part of their burgeoning atomic research program.

Amidst World War IIs turmoil, there was an escalating race to develop weapons. Recognizing the necessity for collaboration, British scientists merged their atomic research efforts with those led by America through the Manhattan Project. Given Fuchs's extensive knowledge and experience in this field, it was only natural that he became a part of this undertaking.

After moving to the United States, he became involved in the core of the project, starting at Columbia University and later at a laboratory called Los Alamos in New Mexico. At Los Alamos, he worked alongside known figures such as Oppenheimer, Fermi, and Teller, contributing to the development of the atomic bomb.

However, beneath his appearance as a scientist was a man grappling with conflicting ideologies. Fuchs's communist beliefs remained strong. As the war progressed, he became increasingly worried about how power would be balanced after it ended. Fearing a future where only the United States possessed atomic weapons supremacy, Fuchs made a life-changing choice. He secretly contacted intelligence and shared vital information about the bomb's design and capabilities.

For years Fuchs managed to keep his life hidden without detection. It wasn't until the 1940s, when new counterintelligence techniques emerged, and key informants defected, that authorities began closing in on him. In 1950 confronted with mounting evidence against him, Fuchs admitted to his acts of espionage. His confession sent shockwaves through intelligence communities alike.

The trial and subsequent imprisonment of Fuchs in Britain gained attention serving as a reminder of the vulnerabilities that exist in a world filled with secrecy and suspicion. Fuchs's motives, driven by beliefs and fear, shed light on the nature of the atomic age, where individual convictions often clashed with national loyalties. Fuchs's betrayal was deeply personal for many, including those who had worked closely with him shattered their trust, emphasizing the stakes during the Cold War era.

In espionage, Klaus Fuchs remains a figure that sparks intrigue and ongoing debate. His story encompasses elements of science, ideology, and betrayal – capturing the dilemmas a world teetering on the edge of the age faces.

The Shadow over Oppenheimer: Accusations and Trials:

During the 1950s, as the Cold War escalated, J. Robert Oppenheimer found himself amid political and ideological upheaval. Once hailed as a hero for his leadership in the Manhattan Project, he now faced allegations that aimed to tarnish his reputation and diminish his contributions to science and national security.

The seeds of doubt had been sown long before the formal hearings took place in 1954. Oppenheimer's past associations his connections with leading organizations and individuals during the 1930s became a focal point for those who opposed him. Additionally, his vocal stance on disarmament after World War II and reservations regarding the development of the hydrogen bomb further distanced him from figures within military and political circles. These disagreements were not solely based on strategic matters; they were deeply rooted in differences that reflected broader divisions prevalent during the Cold War era.

The climax of these tensions occurred in December 1953 when Oppenheimer's security clearance was suspended pending a review. The subsequent hearings by the Atomic Energy Commissions Personnel Security Board became a spectacle that captured attention. Over weeks witnesses were summoned for testimonies. Every aspect of Oppenheimer's life and career underwent meticulous scrutiny.

Former colleagues, friends, and even family members found themselves caught up during the controversy surrounding J. Robert Oppenheimer. Some stood by his integrity and loyalty, while others raised concerns about his judgment and connections.

At the core of the hearings lay a question; Was J. Robert Oppenheimer dependable when it came to safeguarding the nation's sensitive secrets? While he was not directly accused of espionage or treason, some insinuations and hints couldn't be ignored. The proceedings focused not only on Oppenheimer's actions but delved into his character and beliefs. The shadow of the Rosenberg trial and revelations about Klaus Fuchs cast a shadow fostering an atmosphere rife with fear and mistrust.

Oppenheimer maintained his poise throughout the hearings, responding to questions with honesty and reserve. However, it was clear that this took a toll on him. The final blow came in June 1954 when the AEC upheld their decision to revoke his security clearance. Oppenheimer was not only considered disloyal; he was deemed a "security risk" due to his affiliations and temperament.

The Oppenheimer hearings transcended being a tragedy for one man; they served as a reflection of their times. In an era dominated by McCarthyism, Red Scare, and fears regarding espionage, boundaries between loyalty and dissent were constantly shifting.

Oppenheimer's experience served as a reminder of how one's reputation can be damaged and the challenges involved in navigating the complicated realm of Cold War politics.

In the aftermath, both the scientific community and the general public struggled to understand what the Oppenheimer case meant. Despite his contributions to physics and his involvement in the Manhattan Project, the hearings cast a shadow that led to uneasy discussions about how science, ethics, and politics intersected during the atomic age.

Espionage Beyond Borders: Global Intrigues:

The world of espionage was extensive, stretching beyond the borders of the United States. As the Cold War grew more intense, countries engaged in maneuvers on the stage to gain an advantage in the nuclear arms race. The stakes were high. Those involved were willing to risk everything for a slight edge.

In the United Kingdom, prestigious research institutions whispered secrets that traveled across distances. The Cambridge Spy Ring, composed of individuals like Kim Philby and Donald Maclean, showcased how deeply infiltration had taken root. These individuals had embedded themselves within society and shared invaluable information with the Soviets, compromising not only atomic secrets but also NATO strategies and intelligence operations.

Canada became a point of intrigue due to its uranium deposits—the Soviet spy network aimed to extract resources and information to strengthen their capabilities. The Gouzenko Affair uncovered an espionage ring in Canada involving Igor Gouzenko, a cipher clerk. His defection and the documents he provided exposed spies revealing how extensively Soviet operations had infiltrated North America.

Even Australia was not immune to the shadows of espionage. Due to its proximity to Asia and its alliance with powers, Australia became a strategic location. Soviet intelligence agencies recognized the opportunity to gather information on programs and policies in the Asia Pacific region by infiltrating the Australian bureaucracy. The Petrov Affair, which involved the defection of Soviet spies Vladimir and Evdokia Petrov, exposed the web of espionage that had entangled the area.

Torn apart by war divisions and overshadowed by the Iron Curtain, Europe was a hub for espionage activities. East and West engaged in a game of cat and mouse centered around Berlin. This relentless pursuit involved scientists, diplomats, and even ordinary citizens caught up in a world of secrecy and deception. The divided city of Berlin perfectly embodied the era's tension and drama with its operations, tunnel excavations, and clandestine border crossings.

In this interconnected realm of espionage, information held immense value as currency. Nations were willing to blur boundaries and compromise their principles in pursuing nuclear supremacy. The stories of spies, double agents, and defectors spanned across continents and cultures, underscoring the nature of the Cold War conflict.

It wasn't about using weapons; also about using intelligence. The war occurred in research laboratories, diplomatic areas, and secretive streets. The complex game of spying and countering each other's moves on the world stage showed how far countries were willing to go to safeguard their classified information and uncover the secrets of their opponents.

The Price of Paranoia:

The Cold War impacted research as political maneuverings and covert operations created a complex environment. The field of science became a battleground not for intellect but also ideology and influence. Due to its implications for power dynamics, research in this field became a prime target for espionage leading to an atmosphere of mistrust where every association and utterance was carefully analyzed for hidden meanings.

Scientists faced challenges during this era. The pursuit of knowledge, once considered noble and unrestricted, became entangled in agendas and nationalistic fervor. The open exchange of ideas crucial to progress was replaced by secrecy and isolated working environments. Collaborations, previously celebrated as a means to advance knowledge, were now met with suspicion as the lines between allies and adversaries blurred.

J. Robert Oppenheimer, a figure in the world of physics, found himself at the center of this period. His contributions to the Manhattan Project had already secured his place in history books. However, the post-war era brought challenges, shifting alliances, and growing paranoia.

Oppenheimer's past connections, outspoken position on disarmament, and interactions with scientists within the country and internationally were thoroughly examined. The hearings in 1954 aimed at assessing his loyalty were indicative of the prevailing ethos of that era. We witnessed a man whose groundbreaking work had reshaped history, now defending not his achievements but his very character and integrity.

However, the consequences of this atmosphere of paranoia were not limited to individuals like Oppenheimer. The scientific community as a whole grappled with the aftermath. The climate of distrust hindered innovation as researchers became hesitant to share their discoveries. Collaborations among nations declined as they tightened control over research due to fears of espionage. Science, which thrives on curiosity, exploration, and collaboration, was under attack.

In hindsight, the real-life tales of spies and intrigues during the Cold War serve as a warning. They highlight the balance between security and scientific freedom, safeguarding secrets, and fostering collaboration. As we ponder this period in history, it is crucial to remember those individuals who navigated through this landscape—acknowledging their contributions while recognizing the dilemmas they faced and appreciating their enduring legacy.

In their tales, we discover teachings that still hold significance today. These stories serve as a reminder of the strength of curiosity and resilience.

CHAPTER 5: SCIENTIFIC COLLABORATIONS AND RIVALRIES.

Few individuals in history have had as profound an impact as J. Robert Oppenheimer. His brilliance was unquestionable. Equally important were the connections he established with the scientists of his time. These connections, characterized by collaboration, competition, and intense rivalry, played a role in influencing the direction of physics in the 20th century.

Collaborations: The Building Blocks of Discovery:

Oppenheimer's journey into the realm of physics was not defined by his exceptional individual brilliance but also by the intellectual collaborations he cultivated. These partnerships, often formed through exploration, played a crucial role in shaping his scientific perspectives and contributions.

During his academic years, especially while working at the University of California Berkeley and the California Institute of Technology, Oppenheimer was surrounded by a community of budding physicists. This environment buzzed with conversations, debates, and shared aspirations. It was here that Oppenheimer truly grasped the significance of research. By collaborating with scientists, he engaged in discussions where ideas were challenged and refined, ultimately leading to a deeper comprehension of intricate theories.

One of the collaborations in Oppenheimer's career occurred during his time in Europe when he partnered with Max Born—an esteemed physicist. He recognized Oppenheimer's potential at a young age. Their partnership brought together experience and youthful enthusiasm as they delved into the complexities of quantum theory. Each contributed their perspectives to their explorations which resulted in significant advancements within the field—particularly enhancing our understanding of wave functions and quantum states.

However, the collaboration between Born and Oppenheimer went beyond the results. Their relationship extended beyond the confines of the laboratory, characterized by respect and admiration. Born often regarded Oppenheimer as one of his students, testifying to their strong bond on both intellectual and personal levels.

As Oppenheimer's career progressed, his collaborative endeavors expanded further. He became a figure attracting physicists from around the world. Regardless of where his office was located, it served as a center of activity. Students, colleagues, and visiting scientists would gather there frequently for discussions that could stretch on for hours. These informal interactions formed the foundation for groundbreaking discoveries. They exemplified Oppenheimer's belief in pursuing knowledge, where ideas were freely shared, and innovation was an effort.

When we contemplate Oppenheimer's collaborations, it becomes clear that they were more than partnerships. They reflected his philosophy toward both science and life itself. He firmly believed in harnessing wisdom and recognized the magic that arose when brilliant minds came together.

Oppenheimer's collaborations not pushed the boundaries of physics forward. It also played a significant role in shaping a new generation of scientists. He instilled in them the importance of working, fostering discussions, and maintaining an unwavering sense of curiosity.

Rivalries: The Double-Edged Sword:

In 20th-century physics, rivalries were almost as common as collaborations. J. Robert Oppenheimer experienced these rivalries on a level shaping his career trajectory and leaving a lasting impact on his legacy. The intensity of these rivalries reflected the importance of that era when groundbreaking discoveries were being made, and the race to uncover the mysteries of the universe was in swing.

One rivalry that defined Oppenheimer's career was with Edward Teller. Both physicists possessed brilliance and played crucial roles in developing atomic weapons. However, their visions for research diverged significantly. Teller, often called the "father of the hydrogen bomb," staunchly advocated for its advancement. He believed that it was essential for the United States to maintain its superiority given escalating threats.

Conversely, Oppenheimer held reservations about this path. Having witnessed firsthand the power unleashed by bombs, he questioned the morality and necessity of creating an even more destructive weapon. This professional disagreement eventually took a turn when Teller testified against Oppenheimer during his security clearance hearings in 1954—a moment that strained their relationship significantly.
It represented a rivalry that showcased the challenges faced during the age when scientific progress often clashed with moral considerations.

Another noteworthy competition occurred between Richard Feynman and Oppenheimer, physicists who collaborated on the Manhattan Project. However, an underlying tension existed between them. Feynman, known for his approach to physics and inclination to question established norms, frequently found himself at odds with Oppenheimer's traditional viewpoint. While their disagreements were not as widely publicized as those with

Teller, they symbolized the debates taking place within the community. It was a time of change when physicists grappled with theories and discoveries—conflicting opinions were bound to arise.

These rivalries exerted an influence on Oppenheimer's journey. They compelled him to refine his theories and beliefs through challenges. Additionally, these rivalries shed light on the complexities of that era when distinguishing between friends and foes became increasingly blurred. These competitions reflected the tensions experienced in the 20th century—a period marked by hopeful prospects from scientific breakthroughs and profound ethical dilemmas.

The Interplay of Collaboration and Rivalry:

The dynamic interaction between collaboration and rivalry in Oppenheimer's life was truly intriguing. It presented a captivating contrast that showcased his belief in the power of knowledge and the challenges posed by competing ambitions. From the outset, Oppenheimer recognized that the complexities of physics necessitated a pooling of resources leading him to engage in fruitful collaborations with esteemed figures like Max Born. Their joint efforts yielded groundbreaking insights into quantum mechanics, underscoring their shared passion for unraveling the mysteries of our universe.

However, it is important to acknowledge that the world of physics during the 20th century was not devoid of rivalries. While Oppenheimer valued collaboration, he was no stranger to the spirit that often characterizes academia. His differences with contemporaries such as Edward Teller and Richard Feynman extended beyond perspectives and mirrored broader ideological conflicts prevailing at that time. Teller's fervent advocacy for the hydrogen bomb and his involvement in McCarthy-era investigations, including Oppenheimer's security clearance hearings, exemplified how personal vendettas could sometimes disguise themselves as disagreements. Unfortunately, Oppenheimer found himself on the receiving end of these animosities during this era.

But what is truly remarkable is how these two contradictory forces coexisted in Oppenheimer's life. Collaborations and rivalries were like two sides of the coin, each influencing and motivating the other. The competitive atmosphere challenged him to expand his understanding and constantly question, reflect, and refine his theories. Simultaneously the spirit of collaboration allowed him to rise above egos and consider the picture. It was a balancing act that Oppenheimer managed with skill, thanks to his exceptional intelligence and introspection.

This dynamic was evident during Oppenheimer's time at the Institute for Advanced Study in Princeton. He cultivated an environment that nurtured both cooperation and healthy competition. The institute mirrored the community with Oppenheimer ensuring that neither cooperation nor rivalry overshadowed one another. It served as an example of leadership demonstrating how the right blend of collaboration and competition could drive unprecedented scientific progress.

In essence, Oppenheimer's journey reflected the landscape of his era—a landscape where collective knowledge pursuit intertwined with individual aspirations blurring the lines between collaboration and rivalry. It stands as a reminder of how intricate the human mind's countless elements that fuel scientific breakthroughs.

The Symphony of Relationships:

The life of J. Robert Oppenheimer was filled with interactions, where each relationship played a role in shaping his existence. While his scientific accomplishments have received recognition and thorough documentation, the interplay of his personal and professional connections provides a deeper understanding of the man behind the legendary figure.

Collaborations formed melodies within this symphony. They epitomized the pursuit of excellence, minds coming together to unravel the mysteries of the universe. Whether partnering with his mentor Max Born or engaging with intellects at the Institute for Advanced Study in Princeton, Oppenheimer showcased his intellectual brilliance and demonstrated his ability to foster a collective spirit of exploration. These partnerships were more than endeavors; they served as a testament to the strength that unity holds when faced with formidable scientific challenges.

In contrast, disharmonious tones emerged from Oppenheimer's rivalries. These relationships were characterized by tension, competition, and occasional open conflicts. His disagreements with Edward Teller and subtle undercurrents of competition with Richard Feynman exemplified the stakes in 20th-century physics. However, within these rivalries existed a sense of mutual respect—a begrudging admiration for each other's genius. While these rivalries may have caused professional challenges, they also acted as drivers motivating Oppenheimer to achieve even greater accomplishments.

However, viewing Oppenheimer's relationships in terms of collaboration and rivalry would be overly simplistic. Some nuances and complexities defied classification. Some mentors evolved into collaborators, rivals became friends, and friends became critics. Each unique relationship added layers of depth to Oppenheimer's character shaping his perspective and influencing his choices.

Ultimately the interplay of Oppenheimer's relationships provides a glimpse into the workings of one of the mysterious figures of the 20th century. It serves as a reminder that science's fundamentally a human pursuit influenced not only by intellectual endeavors but also by personal interactions. Reflecting on Oppenheimer's life makes us admire the multifaceted connections that defined him.

DRAMATIC RECONSTRUCTIONS OF KEY EVENTS.

The realm of science, often seen as a domain of facts and unbiased truths, is a breeding ground for emotions, ambitions, partnerships, and competitions. J. Robert Oppenheimer's scientific journey was no different. As he navigated the landscape of physics in the century, he encountered allies and adversaries, moments of camaraderie, and instances of conflict. This section delves into some of the retellings of pivotal events that shaped Oppenheimer's collaborations and rivalries.

The Berkeley Years: Collaboration with Ernest O. Lawrence:

During the atmosphere at the University of California Berkeley in the 1930s, two renowned scientists found their paths intersecting. J. Robert Oppenheimer, known for his insights, and Ernest O. Lawrence, a respected experimental physicist, embarked on a collaboration that would shape that era. A shared passion for the emerging field of physics fueled their initial encounters. Lawrence's groundbreaking invention, the cyclotron, revolutionized atomic nucleus research. Oppenheimer recognized its potential as a tool to further his theoretical pursuits. Despite their approaches, they discovered common ground in their aspiration to establish Berkeley as a leading hub for nuclear research.

Over time their collaboration yielded achievements. Joint seminars, research endeavors, and scholarly publications marked their journey. Students and fellow scientists at Berkeley often marveled at their synergy; Lawrence's practical and hands-on approach complemented Oppenheimer's conceptual thinking. Together they transformed the university into a center for research that attracted talent from all corners of the world.

Like any collaboration, differences began to surface, and Lawrence started recognizing applications of reactions beyond scientific exploration.

The allure of energy, with its potential for advancements and industrial applications, deeply fascinated him. However, Oppenheimer remained engrossed in exploring the aspects of physics. Their harmonious brainstorming sessions began to reveal disagreements. Their contrasting visions became particularly apparent when discussing the applications of the cyclotron. While Lawrence envisioned uses, Oppenheimer hesitated to stray far from pure research.

Nevertheless, their strong initial bond ensured that respect endured despite these differences. Their collaborative accomplishments at Berkeley were a testament to the power of teamwork. Even as the world teetered on the brink of war and the Manhattan Project beckoned, Lawrence advocated for Oppenheimer to assume leadership. This recommendation, given by a scientist as esteemed as Lawrence himself, acknowledged their shared history and past triumphs.

In hindsight, the collaboration between Oppenheimer and Lawrence at Berkeley serves as a reminder of the intricacies involved in partnerships. Two brilliant minds driven by shared enthusiasm but guided by visions united to push beyond known boundaries.

Their impact on Berkeley is not limited to the findings they uncovered; it extends to the environment of exploration they nurtured.

The Feynman Conundrum: A Rivalry of Wits:

Amidst the pressure of the Manhattan Project, a unique bond developed between two brilliant minds of the 20th century; J. Robert Oppenheimer and Richard Feynman. Feynman, a physicist with a curiosity and a mischievous streak, brought a fresh and unconventional energy to the project. His approach to physics was intuitive, often challenging established norms and methods. This contrasted sharply with Oppenheimer's philosophical approach to scientific problems.

Their interactions were a mix of admiration and intellectual debates. Feynman's legendary stories about cracking safes and playing pranks on colleagues at Los Alamos added an element of excitement. While entertained by Feynman's antics, Oppenheimer often found himself playing the role of the figure who tempered Feynman's enthusiasm. Their discussions extended beyond physics; they frequently delved into conversations about knowledge, the ethics of scientific exploration, and the associated responsibilities.

One memorable episode highlighting their connection occurred during preparations for the Trinity test. The team faced uncertainties creating an atmosphere of anticipation and anxiety. Feynman lightened the mood by organizing a betting pool on the bomb's expected yield.

Although he didn't actively participate, he understood the significance of the test. For him, the Trinity test went beyond being an experiment; it was a moment that would shape humanity's connection with the atomic age.

As time went by, their paths took directions. Feynman went on to become one of the physicists of his time renowned for his contributions to quantum electrodynamics and his talent for simplifying complex scientific ideas for everyone to understand. Oppenheimer, on the hand, found himself entangled in controversies as he grappled with the ethical and moral implications of his involvement in creating the atomic bomb.

Nevertheless, despite their contrasting experiences, Oppenheimer and Feynman maintained a bond. They held admiration for each other's intellect and contributions. Their relationship serves as a reminder that, at its core, science's an inherently human pursuit influenced by individual personalities, passions, and an unyielding thirst, for knowledge.

The Teller Dilemma: Ideologies at Odds:

In the records of 20th-century physics, few relationships carried as weight and significance as the one between J. Robert Oppenheimer and Edward Teller. They were both figures in their field, but their perspectives on the future of nuclear science and its impact on humanity often clashed.

Edward Teller, a physicist from Hungary, possessed brilliance and an unwavering dedication to nuclear research. However, it was his belief in the necessity of advancing nuclear armaments, particularly the development of the hydrogen bomb, that put him at odds with Oppenheimer. Teller saw the hydrogen bomb, which had more power than the atomic bombs used in Hiroshima and Nagasaki, as a crucial deterrent during the escalating Cold War. He believed the United States needed to maintain superiority in the nuclear arms race due to the looming threat posed by the Soviet Union.

Oppenheimer took an approach; he deeply reflected upon the role of weapons after World War II. The immense devastation caused by bombs weighed heavily on his conscience. As someone who played a role in bringing such a weapon into existence, he grappled with moral and ethical considerations surrounding further advancements in nuclear weaponry.

The concept of the hydrogen bomb, with its potential for destruction, deeply troubled him. Oppenheimer advocated for control over energy and was cautious about entering a new nuclear arms race.

Their differences in ideology were not limited to meetings and scientific conferences. Their disagreements influenced policy and shaped the course of nuclear research in the United States. Teller, pragmatic, openly supported the hydrogen bomb; gained backing from important political and military figures. Oppenheimer, driven by his beliefs, became increasingly isolated in his position.

The climax of their rivalry occurred during the security clearance hearings for Oppenheimer in 1954. Teller's testimony didn't outright condemn Oppenheimer. Raised doubts about his commitment to security. Teller subtly suggested Oppenheimer's opposition to the hydrogen bomb reflected a lack of loyalty. This testimony, coming from a scientist, significantly contributed to Oppenheimer eventually losing his security clearance.

The aftermath of these hearings had reaching consequences. The scientific community became divided as many saw Teller's actions as a betrayal.

Oppenheimer, once hailed as a figure, in the era saw his reputation suffer and his influence in policymaking circles decline. Conversely, Teller persisted in advocating for progress and played a significant role in shaping the U.S. Thermonuclear program.

In hindsight, the rivalry between Oppenheimer and Teller offers a thought-provoking reflection on the interplay of science, ethics, and politics. These brilliant minds, driven by contrasting visions, symbolized the age's debates and dilemmas. Their story serves as a reminder that while pursuing knowledge is commendable, it is accompanied by complexities and consequences that extend beyond laboratory boundaries.

The Dual Nature of Scientific Endeavors:

At its core, science is a quest for knowledge and understanding where we strive to uncover the universe's secrets through investigation and experimentation. It aims to be objective with its methods and findings from biases or emotions. However, when we delve into the world of exploration, we discover that it is intertwined with emotions, ambitions, dreams, and conflicts. The story of J. Robert Oppenheimer serves as a reminder of this interplay.

Oppenheimer's journey in the field of physics was not an endeavor. It was shaped by his interactions with colleagues, mentors, and competitors who brought their perspectives, biases, and personal experiences to the table. These interactions were more than exchanges of data or theories; they were profoundly encounters influenced by individual histories, cultural backgrounds, and personal aspirations. The debates, discussions, and disagreements that marked Oppenheimer's collaborations and rivalries were not about facts but also encompassed personal visions and ethical considerations.

The process of discovery itself is inherently emotional. The exhilaration accompanying an achievement or the frustration experienced when confronted with challenges are deeply relatable human experiences. Additionally, the emergence of technologies often raises dilemmas that elicit emotional responses on a profound level.

Oppenheimer's internal struggles in the aftermath of the bombings of Hiroshima and Nagasaki shed light on the profound moral and ethical dilemmas that scientific advancements can present. His introspection and public stance on disarmament emphasize that while science follows methods, it operates in a world shaped by human values and societal norms.

When contemplating the nature of pursuits, we are reminded of the responsibilities accompanying discovery. Science can reshape our world by introducing novel technologies and questioning established conventions. However, this power necessitates welding—considering the implications of our findings—and engaging in open conversations about our future path. Oppenheimer's life, characterized by collaborations, rivalries, accomplishments, and hurdles, stands as evidence of how intertwined science's with humanity. It encourages us to perceive endeavors not as a quest for objective truth but as an inherently human journey filled with complexities, joys, and dilemmas that define our shared human experience.

Chapter 6: Oppenheimer in Popular Culture.

J. Robert Oppenheimer, a figure in the field of science, has surpassed the boundaries of scholarly publications and historical accounts to become a revered symbol in popular culture. His life, characterized by brilliance, controversy, and self-reflection, has inspired portrayals across media outlets. This section delves into how Oppenheimer has been depicted in culture, examining the interpretations and reimaginations of the man, the scientist, and the legendary persona that have captivated public interest.

The Silver Screen's Scientist:

Hollywood's appeal lies in its ability to amplify, intensify and immortalize real-life individuals. The cinematic portrayals of J. Robert Oppenheimer are an example of this phenomenon. Oppenheimer's character is complex, marked by his intellect dilemmas and personal struggles, making it a captivating subject for filmmakers to explore. Throughout the years, various interpretations of Oppenheimer have graced the silver screen, each shedding light on aspects of his life and legacy.

One noteworthy depiction comes from the film "Fat Man and Little Boy" (1989). Set against the backdrop of the Manhattan Project during World War II, this movie delves into the high-pressure atmosphere at Los Alamos. Dwight Schultz delivers a portrayal of Oppenheimer. The film captures the scientist's enthusiasm for the project, driven by the urgency of war and the exhilaration of discovery. However, as the story unfolds, we witness Oppenheimer grappling with conflict. The realization of the bomb's potential and subsequent use in Hiroshima and Nagasaki weigh heavily on him, prompting introspection and moral questioning. While "Fat Man and Little Boy" takes some liberties expected in films, it succeeds in presenting a dimensional

Oppenheimer who finds himself torn between his duties as a scientist and his conscience as a human being.

Oppenheimer's influence extends beyond being portrayed in films. It can also be seen in movies that explore themes such as power, war, and ethics. Although the characters may not directly represent Oppenheimer himself, they often embody the struggles of individuals grappling with the consequences of their creations. Whether focused on Oppenheimer or inspired by him, these cinematic interpretations mirror society's feelings toward progress. They raise questions about the responsibilities of scientists, the boundaries of discovery, and the costs associated with progress.

Ultimately Hollywood's fascination with Oppenheimer serves as a testament to his lasting impact on our consciousness. His life story, filled with brilliance and tragedy, provides filmmakers with a narrative brimming with tension, drama, and introspection. Through film as a medium, audiences are encouraged to contemplate not the man himself and his choices but the broader implications of scientific advancements in our modern era.

Television's Take:

Television has frequently directed its attention toward J. Robert Oppenheimer, utilizing its narrative capabilities to provide viewers with an in-depth and personal exploration of his life and legacy. The episodic nature of this medium allows for a portrayal that captures the complexities of Oppenheimer's character and the era he lived in.

One notable television depiction of Oppenheimer was seen in the BBC series "Oppenheimer" in 1980. Starring Sam Waterston as the character, the series spanned seven episodes, each delving into phases of his life. From his days as a student fascinated by quantum mechanics to his pivotal role in leading the Manhattan

Project and finally to the political and ethical challenges he faced later on, no aspect was left unexplored. Waterston's performance deserves mention for portraying Oppenheimer's internal conflicts and moral dilemmas. Additionally, the series did not shy away from illustrating his hardships, including relationships and battles with depression.

Television's portrayal of Oppenheimer also reflects society's evolving perceptions during the age. In episodes focusing on the Manhattan Project, viewers can sense both excitement and urgency surrounding efforts, alongside concerns regarding creating such a devastating weapon. The series also explores the maneuvering of that time, highlighting the tensions between exploration and government oversight.

Television as a medium allows for interaction with its audience. Episodes often conclude with moments prompting viewers to contemplate the decisions made by Oppenheimer and his team while eagerly anticipating the installment to witness the consequences of those choices. This recurring suspense reflects the real-life excitement and unpredictability surrounding discoveries and political intrigues.

Apart from the BBC series, various documentaries and historical programs have touched upon Oppenheimer's life. Although these programs may not solely focus on him, they frequently emphasize his contributions and the ethical debates surrounding the bomb. Through interviews, archival footage, and expert commentary, television ensures that Oppenheimer's legacy remains a subject of discussion, debate, and introspection for generations.

Essentially television's depiction of J. Robert Oppenheimer extends beyond a retelling of events; it offers an immersive experience. It invites viewers to step into his shoes, grapple with the challenges he encountered, and ponder on the implications of discovery within society's values and ethical frameworks.

Literary Interpretations:

The intriguing persona of J. Robert Oppenheimer has long fascinated the world of literature. His life, characterized by his prowess in ethical dilemmas and personal challenges, offers a rich foundation for exploration. Biographies, although providing narratives, often delve into his psyche in an attempt to unravel the intricacies that defined him. Among these works, " Prometheus; The Triumph and Tragedy of J. Robert Oppenheimer" by Kai Bird and Martin J. Sherwin stands out. Through research and compelling storytelling, the authors paint a dimensional picture of Oppenheimer—capturing his brilliance, leadership during the Manhattan Project, and the subsequent trials that marred his reputation.

Works of fiction—sometimes indirectly referencing him—have been inspired by the themes and challenges he faced in life. With its promises and perils, the atomic era has provided a backdrop for novels throughout the century. Characters resembling Oppenheimer wrestle with the implications of their pursuits—an echo of his real-life struggles. These literary interpretations frequently delve into inquiries about the timeless conflict between knowledge and responsibility, creation and destruction.

Even poetry finds inspiration in Oppenheimer's story. J. Robert Oppenheimer's deep reflections and contemplation influenced by the Bhagavad Gita during the Trinity test sparked the creation of poems. These verses often express admiration for Oppenheimer as a scientist and despair over the power he unleashed. The contrasting aspects of Oppenheimer's legacy being both a creator and a destroyer serve as a recurring theme that provides poets with a wealth of emotions and imagery to explore.

Oppenheimer's life has also found its way onto the stage through adaptations. The ethical dilemmas, intrigues, and personal challenges he faced offer material to create tension on stage. Characters inspired by him grapple with their consciences, confront judgment and navigate complex corridors of power and politics. Although these plays are grounded in events, they often draw parallels to issues ensuring that Oppenheimer's story remains relevant today just as it was during his lifetime.

Ultimately, the world's fascination with J. Robert Oppenheimer is evidence of his universally relatable journey. While his life was extraordinary, it touches upon themes that resonate with all individuals; the pursuit of knowledge, the weight of responsibility, and the eternal quest, for redemption. Through their written works, authors, poets, and playwrights ensure that Oppenheimer's multifaceted legacy continues to inspire and challenge generations.

Artistic Representations:

The enigmatic personality of J. Robert Oppenheimer, with its combination of brilliance, inner conflict, and introspection, has long fascinated the community. Artists across mediums have been intrigued by capturing the essence of a man who stood at the crossroads of groundbreaking discoveries and profound ethical challenges.

In art, painters have frequently been drawn to depicting Oppenheimer's face. His contemplative gaze, immortalized in photographs from the era of the Manhattan Project, has been reimagined on canvases. Some artists portray him against a backdrop featuring a mushroom cloud—a reminder of the power of atomic bombs. These paintings often contrast Oppenheimer's reflective demeanor with the unrestrained energy of the explosion fostering a dialogue between the creator and his creation.

Sculptures have also sought to capture Oppenheimer's legacy. Bronze and stone effigies found in institutions depict the physicist lost in profound thought. These statues, often life-sized, invite observers to contemplate both the man himself and his contributions. They stand as testaments to Oppenheimer's enduring impact on science and society.

In addition to art forms, contemporary installations have explored Oppenheimer's life and legacy. Exhibits that incorporate forms of media, such as clips, videos, and interactive elements, offer a comprehensive experience. When people visit these displays in museums and galleries, they are often fully immersed in a journey. They start by exploring Oppenheimer's years, then move through the intense days of the Manhattan Project to finally reflect on the atomic age. These installations challenge viewers by making them confront the moral dilemmas Oppenheimer grappled with.

Oppenheimer's influence has also left its mark on performance arts. Experimental theater productions have brought moments from his life to life on stage, blending accuracy with artistic interpretation. Through dance performances, dancers have conveyed the emotions that defined Oppenheimer's journey. Dances fluidity allows it to express a range of emotions enabling it to portray Oppenheimer's conflicts, moments of joy, and deep introspection that shaped his life.

In essence, artistic representations of J. Robert Oppenheimer are as diverse and intricate as the man himself. Artists from mediums and genres have been captivated by his story. Seek to capture the subtleties of his life journey through their works. Through these creations, they encourage us to reflect upon, question, and understand the person behind the legend while reminding us of how individuals can impact history.

Music and Musings:

J. Robert Oppenheimer has left an impact on both the ethical realms, which has resonated deeply within the world of music. His complex personality, coupled with the implications of his work, has provided ground for musicians to explore, interpret and express their artistry. Oppenheimer's influence looms large from compositions to rock, often serving as a source of inspiration for introspection and social commentary.

One powerful reference to Oppenheimer in music can be found in his words from the Bhagavad Gita; "Now I am become Death, the destroyer of worlds." This statement was uttered in the aftermath of the Trinity test. Encapsulates the nature of creation and destruction. Numerous musicians across genres and generations have incorporated this quote or its essence into their lyrics, using it as a metaphor to address various societal issues such as war and peace, personal struggles, and triumphs.

Furthermore, Oppenheimer's enduring legacy has also deeply influenced classical music. Composers have been drawn to the depth and philosophical significance of his journey. Operas like John Adam's "Doctor Atomic," symphonies, and chamber pieces have sought to capture the essence of Oppenheimer and the atomic age he was instrumental in shaping.

The opera explores the moments leading up to the Trinity test focusing on Oppenheimer as the figure. Adam's composition effectively captures the emotions, excitement, and ethical dilemmas of that moment. Oppenheimer's character frequently engages in solo performances contemplating the nature of his work and its reaching consequences.

In the realm of rock and pop music, Oppenheimer's impact is more. Equally profound. Numerous bands have incorporated imagery of the bomb and its connection to Oppenheimer to highlight affairs, the fragility of peace, and the responsibilities accompanying power. The atomic age, with Oppenheimer at its core, provides a backdrop for songs that touch upon themes such as love, loss, hope, and despair.

Beyond notes and lyrics, broader cultural reflections inspired by Oppenheimer are evident in album artwork, music videos, and stage performances. Visual representations often take symbolic forms in tandem with the music to create an experience for audiences. The iconic mushroom cloud serves as a haunting reminder of the power wielded by bombs; it frequently appears throughout various artistic expressions alongside superimposed images or silhouettes of Oppenheimer himself—adding layers of meaning and allowing for diverse interpretations.

J. Robert Oppenheimer's life was characterized by his brilliance, nature, and deep introspection. Enough, his impact has not reverberated in the scientific community but also in music. Musicians have taken inspiration from his life experiences to create compositions that delve into aspects of humanity, such as our boundaries, the essence of discovery, and the ethical dilemmas we face.

The Digital Age's Depiction:

In this era of progress and the widespread use of the internet, J. Robert Oppenheimer's legacy has found new meaning and resonance among the younger generation. With its platforms and global audiences, the digital world has become a space for exploring and sharing Oppenheimer's life and contributions.

The emergence of documentaries and web series has revolutionized how we tell stories. Platforms like YouTube and

Vimeo now host a wealth of content dedicated to Oppenheimer, presenting a view of his accomplishments and the ethical dilemmas he faced. These digital narratives often incorporate archival footage interviews with experts and insightful analyses that offer viewers an understanding of Oppenheimer's impact on society. These platforms enable viewers worldwide to engage in discussions by sharing their thoughts, asking questions, and participating in debates about Oppenheimer's influence on our world.

Additionally, podcasts have emerged as a form of storytelling in this age. Episodes dedicated to Oppenheimer delve into details about his life by featuring interviews with experts, historians, and even family members. The intimate nature of podcast conversations allows hosts and guests to delve deeply into discussions that offer listeners insights into Oppenheimer's personality beyond what's found in textbooks.

Social media platforms, like Twitter and Instagram, have played a role in keeping J. Robert Oppenheimer's legacy alive. On anniversaries such as the Trinity test or the Hiroshima bombing, dedicated posts and discussions about Oppenheimer emerge, reflecting on his quotes, the ethical dilemmas he faced, and the wider impact of nuclear power. These platforms, known for their concise content and visual appeal, introduce Oppenheimer to audiences who may be encountering him for the time.

However, not just conversations and historical reflections dominate Oppenheimer's presence. The internet, with its sense of humor and love for memes, has found ways to embrace Oppenheimer. His quote, "Now I am become Death, the destroyer of worlds," has been repurposed, remixed, and transformed into memes, GIFs, and digital artwork pieces. Some use it to comment on issues, while others employ it in contexts to showcase the versatility of digital culture.

J. Robert Oppenheimer's legacy remains vibrant and relevant thanks to the age. Through platforms and creative storytelling techniques, his life and contributions continue to inspire curiosity and provoke thoughtful discussions among internet users worldwide.

The world of technology has found a way to preserve Oppenheimer's legacy guaranteeing that his story will be shared and passed down through the ages.

The Cultural Echo of a Scientific Titan:

J. Robert Oppenheimer left an enduring mark on history that extends beyond science and academia. His impact can be felt in forms of culture, including films, literature, art, and digital media. While these portrayals differ in their interpretations, they all converge on a theme; the influence of one man's journey through the tumultuous landscape of 20th-century science. Oppenheimer's transformation into an icon serves as a reminder of how individual brilliance and societal reflection are intricately connected. His life, marked by brilliance, controversy, and introspection, continues to inspire and captivate, ensuring that the legend of Oppenheimer lives on in the consciousness of generations.

VISUAL GALLERY OF MEDIA PORTRAYALS

The rich culture surrounding J. Robert Oppenheimer is as complex and fascinating as the man himself. In this section, we'll explore portrayals of Oppenheimer in culture, providing readers with a vivid and descriptive collection that captures the different interpretations and lasting impact of his legacy.

Cinematic Glimpses: Beyond the Biopic:

The film industry's fascination with J. Robert Oppenheimer goes beyond the retellings of his life story. While traditional biographical movies have portrayed the man exploring his professional life, filmmakers have also explored more abstract and symbolic interpretations of Oppenheimer. His character has served as a lens through which broader themes of science, ethics, and humanity are explored.

In cinema, Oppenheimer's character has been used as a figure. His silhouette, set against the backdrop of a mushroom cloud, has become an image that captures the dual nature of human achievement and its potential for destruction. These films often rely on visuals and soundscapes than dialogue or narrative to convey the profound consequences of the atomic age. They challenge viewers to grapple with the dilemmas that Oppenheimer himself faced.

On the hand, independent filmmakers have taken liberties to reimagine different stages of Oppenheimer's life. Some have created histories speculating on "what if" scenarios. What if Oppenheimer had walked away from the Manhattan Project? What if he had become an advocate for disarmament earlier in his career? Although fictional, these films provide insights into the paths that Oppenheimer's life could have followed.

Oppenheimer's story has captivated filmmakers from cultures and backgrounds, resulting in various interpretations in international cinema. Each filmmaker brings their perspective to the table depicting Oppenheimer as a hero entangled in the complexities of war and politics or as a representation of the eternal struggle between duty and conscience. These varied portrayals highlight the nature of Oppenheimer's dilemmas. Emphasize the global significance of his contributions.

With its array of tools and techniques, the realm of cinema has successfully presented a dimensional depiction of J. Robert

Oppenheimer. By blending elements with storytelling, symbolism, and creative interpretation, filmmakers have ensured that Oppenheimer's legacy remains deeply embedded in the collective consciousness of audiences worldwide.

Graphic Novels and Illustrations: A Different Shade of Ink:

The realm of novels presents a captivating means to delve into the life and impact of J. Robert Oppenheimer, blending storytelling and narrative depth. Unlike biographies that rely on text, graphic novels utilize illustrations to portray historical events vividly. This art form, often associated with superheroes and fantasy stories, has emerged as a tool for recounting history and biography. Oppenheimer's complex persona and dramatic experiences offer grounds for creative pursuits.

The collaboration between artists and writers in these projects poses the challenge of simplifying concepts and historical occurrences while maintaining accessibility and engagement. The Manhattan Project comes alive through the illustrator's hand with its array of characters, covert operations, and groundbreaking discoveries. Detailed scenes depicting bustling laboratories in Los Alamos with scientists poring over blueprints or the foreboding silhouette of the atomic bomb showcase attention to detail. The chosen color palettes often convey the mood of that era; sepia tones capture a feel from the 20th century, while stark blacks and reds evoke the tension and urgency of wartime.

However, it is not events that find their place within these pages. Intimate glimpses into Oppenheimer's life, whether it's his moments in his study or casual interactions with colleagues, are portrayed with a sensitive touch that allows readers to get to know the man behind the legend. The conversations, often inspired by letters, speeches, and documents, add authenticity to the storytelling.

Graphic novels offer a platform where artists can take liberties. Some creators choose to blend accounts with symbolic sequences. For example, Oppenheimer's inner conflict after the Trinity test might be depicted through dream scenes where he faces the implications of his work. Though not biographical, these artistic choices provide insights into Oppenheimer's mindset.

Illustrations have also played a role outside novels in shaping how people perceive Oppenheimer. Iconic photographs of the physicist lost in thought or delivering a lecture have inspired interpretations. Whether they are portraits or abstract depictions, these illustrations capture Oppenheimer's essence—showcasing his intelligence, charisma, and profound influence on history.

In storytelling, J. Robert Oppenheimer's life stands as evidence of the arts' ability to educate and inspire emotions. Leave an impact.
His legacy is beautifully portrayed in the pages of novels and illustrations, creating a connection between the past and present. It also encourages the generation to contemplate his contributions and their impact.

Interactive Exhibitions: Walk Through History:

In the revered halls of museums and cultural institutions, the enduring legacy of J. Robert Oppenheimer unfolds in an immersive way. These captivating exhibits, carefully curated, offer visitors a voyage into the life and era of the man often hailed as the "Father of the Atomic Bomb."

Upon stepping into these exhibits, one is instantly transported to the century. The air is filled with sounds—a blend of 1920s jazz and hushed academic conversations, setting a nostalgic ambiance. Immaculate replicas of Oppenheimer's study, with his cherished books, handwritten notes, and occasional coffee stains, forge a tangible connection to this esteemed physicist. Visitors can sit at his desk and peruse replicas of his papers. Briefly walk in the shoes of this luminary.

However, it's not solely artifacts that captivate audiences. State-of-the-art technology plays a role in these exhibitions. Reality (AR) stations equipped with glasses seamlessly overlay digital information onto real-life objects. For instance, by viewing a diary through these glasses, animated sketches might bring Oppenheimer's thought processes to life as he grappled with equations.

Virtual reality (VR) booths take visitors on a journey to moments in Oppenheimer's life, such as the streets of his childhood in New York City or the intense atmosphere of the Los Alamos laboratory during the Manhattan Project.

One of the features of these exhibitions is a timeline that covers entire walls. This technological wonder allows visitors to explore Oppenheimer's life year by year. By touching panels, they can uncover photographs, personal letters, and even audio recordings. Visitors can listen to Oppenheimer's lectures, witness his debates with scientists, and ponder his thoughts on the ethical implications of his groundbreaking work.

Another captivating aspect is a recreation of the Trinity test. Through a combination of projections and surround sound, visitors can experience a scaled-down version of the ever-nuclear explosion. This awe-inspiring experience is accompanied by Oppenheimer's words serving as a reminder to attendees about the responsibility that comes with scientific discovery.

As visitors conclude their journey, they are often greeted with a space to jot down their thoughts, emotions, and reflections on Oppenheimer's life and enduring legacy.

These messages, often shown on a wall, create a changing display of public thoughts, ensuring the discussion about Oppenheimer's achievements stays lively and significant.

Essentially these interactive displays go beyond being exhibitions of Oppenheimer's life. They offer experiences that merge the past and present, encouraging visitors to gain knowledge about the physicist and also delve into the intricacies and subtleties of his lasting impact.

Digital Art and Animation: The Modern Tribute:

In today's age, where screens dominate our lives, J. Robert Oppenheimer's legacy has found a vibrant outlet on the digital canvas. Digital art has opened up possibilities for artists to reimagine and reinterpret Oppenheimer's life in once unimaginable ways. Through paintings, artists capture the intensity of Oppenheimer's gaze, often juxtaposing it against ethereal backgrounds of galaxies, atomic structures, or abstract representations of time and space. These artworks are shared on platforms like DeviantArt or ArtStation, blending reverence with modern aesthetics and resonating with a generation that didn't experience the Atomic Age firsthand.

Oppenheimer's story has also found its place in animated shorts that harness the storytelling capabilities of animation. Available on platforms like YouTube, these animations explore aspects of his life. Some delve into the turmoil he faced during the Manhattan Project using visuals and soundscapes to convey the weightiness of his decisions. Others take an approach by simplifying scientific concepts related to Oppenheimer's work through animation, making them accessible to students and curious individuals.

The realm of digital artistry extends beyond images and animations alone.

Interactive digital experiences, such as augmented reality (AR) apps, have been developed to provide users with ways to engage with Oppenheimer's story. Just imagine pointing your smartphone at an area and suddenly witnessing a representation of Oppenheimer himself narrating a chapter from his life or elucidating scientific concepts. These innovative advancements bridge the gap between history and technology, ensuring that Oppenheimer's legacy remains relevant and captivating for the tech generation.

The collaborative nature of the digital art community has resulted in projects paying tribute to Oppenheimer. Collaborative animations, where multiple artists contribute segments or digital art challenges centered around Oppenheimer, have fostered a sense of community. These collaborative endeavors are often accompanied by discussions, critiques, and opportunities for shared learning—showcasing an enduring fascination with Oppenheimer's life and contributions.

In essence, the realm of media has infused vitality into Oppenheimer's legacy. Through pixels, vectors, and code, a new generation of artists and storytellers ensures that J. Robert Oppenheimer's story continues to inspire, intrigue, and captivate audiences worldwide.

Fashion and Pop Art: The Unexpected Canvas:

In the streets of city centers and the innovative halls of art galleries, a homage to J. Robert Oppenheimer emerges. The world of fashion and pop art, which may seem distant from the realms of research, has embraced Oppenheimer unexpectedly and profoundly.

Fashion can reflect sentiments through its ever-changing trends. In recent years, there has been a trend of incorporating iconic historical figures into wearable art. Artists have utilized t-shirts, jackets, and footwear as canvases to showcase Oppenheimer's face. However, it goes beyond putting his image on fabric. These designs often juxtapose Oppenheimer's visage with symbols creating a dialogue between the past and present. For example, one popular design merges his silhouette with neon graphics of 80s pop culture, suggesting his influence across generations.

Pop art—a movement known for blurring the boundaries between art and popular culture—has also found inspiration in Oppenheimer. Artists have reimagined him using colors influenced by figures like Andy Warhol and Roy Lichtenstein. These artworks are frequently exhibited in galleries, displayed as street murals capturing Oppenheimer's various moods and settings.

You may stumble upon a piece where he is depicted amidst book explosions paying homage to his heritage and the popular culture of the 60s. Another artwork might portray him in a stance, surrounded by patterns that mirror the intricacies of his thoughts and choices.

What drives this fascination with mediums? Perhaps it's the allure of Oppenheimer's paradox. A scientist with the soul of a poet creating a weapon of destruction while advocating for peace. This duality resonates with artists and designers urging them to explore his persona through mediums that are relatable and accessible to the masses. Additionally, in an era dominated by fashion and digital art trends, the enduring presence of Oppenheimer-themed creations suggests a deeper connection that withstands time.

Ultimately blending Oppenheimer's lasting legacy with fashion and pop art highlights a truth; icons transcend their domains, influencing and inspiring in ways we least expect. Through these expressions, Oppenheimer's story, encompassing science, ethics, and humanity, continues to captivate our imagination. It proves that true legends never fade; they merely find platforms to shine.

The Everlasting Echo of Oppenheimer:

The impact of J. Robert Oppenheimer goes beyond the realm of history; it echoes throughout culture, leaving its mark on various forms of artistic expression. This collection of visuals provides a glimpse into the array of portrayals, each capturing a distinct aspect of Oppenheimer's persona, accomplishments, and the profound moral dilemmas he faced. From captivating silver screen adaptations to vibrant artwork, Oppenheimer's story is retold, reimagined, and admired. It is important to acknowledge that as we move forward, even as mediums change and interpretations differ, the essence of Oppenheimer's journey—a tale characterized by brilliance, ethical challenges, and unwavering resilience—remains timeless and universally significant.

CHAPTER 7: THE SCHOLAR AND THE TEACHER.

J. Robert Oppenheimer's impact extends beyond his contributions to the age. Exploring his roles as a scholar and educator is essential to truly grasp his character. This chapter aims to illuminate these known yet important aspects of Oppenheimer's life.

The Scholar: A Lifelong Pursuit of Knowledge:

J. Robert Oppenheimer's intellectual journey was truly remarkable, showing a curiosity that extended beyond the boundaries of education—his time at New York's Ethical Culture School during his years laid the groundwork for a passion for learning. Here, he explored subjects and embraced humanities developing a holistic perspective that influenced him throughout his life.

His exceptional academic skills became evident during his time at Harvard University. Although initially drawn to chemistry, a series of encounters and personal reflections guided him toward the field of physics. However, Oppenheimer's thirst for knowledge went beyond absorbing facts; he wanted to push boundaries, challenge assumptions and unravel the mysteries of the universe. This pursuit led him to Europe, where he immersed himself in the emerging field of quantum mechanics. Guided by figures like Max Born, he delved into its intricacies. Made significant contributions to its foundational theories.

Nevertheless, Oppenheimer's intellectual pursuits were not confined solely to physics. He possessed an appreciation for literature, philosophy, and the arts. He even possessed fluency in Sanskrit. Often drew inspiration from classical texts such as the

Bhagavad Gita. This interdisciplinary approach exemplified his belief that knowledge is interconnected and interdependent.

For him, comprehending the universe went beyond equations and scientific experiments; it involved intertwining the realms of science, art, history, and philosophy.

His return to the United States marked a chapter in his voyage. At institutions like the University of California Berkeley and the California Institute of Technology, he embarked on groundbreaking research in physics. Oppenheimer's work was characterized by a combination of insights and innovative thinking during this period. Whether it was his contributions to quantum field theory or his investigations into phenomena, Oppenheimer's research demonstrated an understanding and a forward-thinking vision for the future of the field.

However, what truly distinguished Oppenheimer was his modesty. Despite his knowledge and accomplishments, he remained receptive to ideas and was always willing to question and be questioned. He believed that knowledge-seeking was a journey than a final destination—this spirit of inquiry and unwavering quest for comprehension defined J. Robert Oppenheimer as a scholar.

The Teacher: Inspiring the Next Generation:

J. Robert Oppenheimer's impact as an educator often goes unnoticed amid his reputation as a physicist. However, those fortunate enough to attend his lectures or engage in discussions with him knew that Oppenheimer was much more than the "Father of the Atomic Bomb." He served as a mentor, a guide, and a true inspiration.

At the core of his teaching philosophy was the belief that education shouldn't be a transfer of knowledge but an active exploration of ideas. Oppenheimer's lectures at Berkeley and Caltech weren't presentations of established theories; they were discussions that encouraged students to question, debate, and think critically. His classroom served as a space where boundaries were constantly pushed, and students weren't learners but contributors to the ever-evolving realm of physics.

Oppenheimer's approach to teaching was groundbreaking due to its nature. He firmly believed that gaining an understanding of physics required embracing perspectives. His lectures incorporated elements from literature, philosophy, history, and even art. Ancient texts often found their way into his teachings as he drew parallels between the mysteries of the universe and existential queries posed by philosophers and poets.
Oppenheimer saw physics as more than equations and experiments; he believed it provided insight into the essence of existence.

But what stood out about Oppenheimer as a teacher was his interest in his student's growth. He would spend hours outside class discussing ideas guiding research and even delving into their aspirations and challenges. Many of his students, who later became figures in physics, often spoke about how Oppenheimer's mentorship shaped their paths. His feedback went beyond simply pointing out mistakes; it aimed to foster curiosity and a pursuit of excellence.

However, being a student under Oppenheimer wasn't always easy. He set expectations and constantly challenged his students. His critiques were sharp but constructive, pushing them to their limits. Within this demanding environment, students found purpose. They learned the principles of physics, developed discipline, perseverance, and a passion for making significant contributions to the field.

In the annals of academia, J. Robert Oppenheimer will be remembered not for his achievements but also his lasting impact as an educator.

He dedicated himself to shaping a wave of physicists fostering their curiosity and dedication to exploring the frontiers of knowledge. His teachings have left an impact, serving as a source of inspiration for students and educators alike.

A Legacy Beyond the Atomic Age:

J. Robert Oppenheimer, often associated with the age, had an influence that went beyond the Manhattan Project and the bombings in Hiroshima and Nagasaki. While these events undoubtedly shaped his life and had impacts, it's crucial to acknowledge his contributions, particularly in academia and mentoring.

Oppenheimer's intellectual pursuits were extensive and diverse. He wasn't a physicist; he was a polymath. His exploration of literature, philosophy, and even ancient languages showcased his curiosity about comprehending the world as a whole. This interdisciplinary approach enriched his understanding and set an example for future generations. He demonstrated that true brilliance lies in connecting fields and uncovering hidden patterns that shape our collective knowledge.

As an educator, Oppenheimer had an effect. He didn't simply teach physics; he fostered a mindset. His lectures were known for their depth and eloquence; they went beyond exercises. They took students' journeys into the subject matter, encouraging them to question, debate, and contemplate deeply. Many of those he mentored went on to establish their positions in the field of science, upholding the legacy of critical thinking and comprehensive comprehension that Oppenheimer advocated for.

However, the perspective he instilled within the scientific community stands out prominently in Oppenheimer's lasting impact. In the aftermath of World War II, as humanity grappled with the implications of power, Oppenheimer emerged as a voice of reason and contemplation. He consistently highlighted the responsibilities that accompanied discoveries urging his colleagues to consider the societal and moral consequences of their work. This ethical lens, which insists upon perceiving science not as a tool but as a force with ramifications, is now more pertinent than ever.

Looking back, although discussions about Oppenheimer often revolve around the age, it is crucial to acknowledge and celebrate how he influenced aspects of our world. His legacy serves as a testament to the power of curiosity, the significance of learning, and the imperative need for deliberations in realms of exploration.

GUEST ESSAYS AND REFLECTIONS.

J. Robert Oppenheimer was more than an intelligent physicist; he also profoundly impacted his students and colleagues as an educator. His unique teaching approach, unwavering love for learning, and talent for motivating others are legendary. In the following section, we'll explore guest essays and personal reflections that provide insight into Oppenheimer's role as an individual and an inspiring teacher.

A Classroom with Oppenheimer: An Unforgettable Experience:

The atmosphere in a lecture hall would transform whenever J. Robert Oppenheimer stepped onto the stage. There was an excitement, a breath-holding as students readied themselves for more than just a lecture; they were embarking on a captivating journey. With each spoken word, Oppenheimer painted images of the enigmas of the universe, making the abstract tangible and the complex understandable. His lectures were not exercises; they were extraordinary lessons in critical thinking, challenging students to question, contemplate and explore.

Oppenheimer's teaching style blended discipline with passionate storytelling. He possessed an ability to interweave philosophical and scientific aspects of a subject matter, offering his students a comprehensive understanding. For Oppenheimer, physics went beyond equations and theories; it was a narrative encompassing curiosity and the relentless pursuit of knowledge. He frequently peppered his lectures with anecdotes from scientists' lives, drawing parallels and emphasizing the elements that led to groundbreaking discoveries.

What truly distinguished Oppenheimer was his approach. He firmly believed that learning should be a two-way street. In lecturing, he actively engaged his audience. He posed thought-provoking questions encouraging students to express their thoughts, uncertainties, and interpretations.

Oppenheimer's teaching approach, reminiscent of the method, ensured his classes were vibrant and interactive. It was not uncommon for a lecture to evolve into a debate skillfully guided by Oppenheimer to maintain an enlightening atmosphere.

Students often praised Oppenheimer's ability to make them feel acknowledged and valued. Despite the lecture hall, he had a knack for establishing personal connections with his audience. He keenly observed their reactions adapting his pace and approach accordingly. If he sensed any confusion or uncertainty, he would revisit concepts, breaking them down further through analogies and examples until that "aha" moment of understanding was unmistakable.

Beyond his brilliance, there was a genuine warmth exuded by Oppenheimer. He genuinely cared about the growth and well-being of his students. After lectures, he frequently stayed behind to engage in one-on-one discussions addressing questions and providing guidance. These interactions proved transformative for students as conversations transcended into valuable life lessons.

In conclusion, being in J. Robert Oppenheimer's classroom meant more than receiving an education; it represented a milestone for aspiring physicists. It was an environment where minds were sharpened, perspectives broadened, and the true essence of education cherished.

Those who were lucky to be his students gained the knowledge he shared and also embraced the core principles of his teaching philosophy; an emphasis on curiosity, critical thinking, and the sheer delight of exploration.

The Legacy of His Pedagogy:

J. Robert Oppenheimer had a teaching style that combined traditional methods with approaches. While he valued the importance of knowledge in his teaching, he also embraced the evolving trends in education that emphasized thinking and holistic understanding. His classrooms were not just spaces for memorization; they served as arenas for exploration. Each lecture and discussion was an opportunity to delve into the subject matter to question, challenge and ultimately discover insights.

Oppenheimer's impact on curriculum development was profound. At institutions like the California Institute of Technology and the University of California Berkeley, he shaped academic programs that balanced rigor and breadth. He believed a genuine understanding of physics could not exist in isolation; it needed to be interwoven with perspectives from philosophy, literature, history, and other disciplines. This interdisciplinary approach was groundbreaking at the time as it challenged structures and fostered a more comprehensive grasp of the subject.

However, one aspect of Oppenheimer's teaching philosophy stood out as enduring; his emphasis on learning. He believed true comprehension came from hands-on engagement rather than passive listening or reading alone. As a result, he placed importance on laboratory work, research projects, and field studies to provide students with experiences.

Students were free to explore and put theories to the test in real-world situations and learn from successes and failures. This hands-on approach made complex concepts more understandable and relatable.

Mentorship played a role in Oppenheimer's philosophy. He saw himself not as a teacher but as a guide, mentor, and sometimes even a friend. He dedicated time to truly understand his student's aspirations, strengths, and weaknesses providing guidance that extended beyond academics. Many of his students, who went on to achieve things themselves, often fondly recalled the countless hours spent in Oppenheimer's office discussing physics and life's big questions, dreams, and what lay ahead.

Looking back now, Oppenheimer's teaching methods hold timeless significance. In today's evolving educational landscape, the fundamental principles he advocated for— interdisciplinary learning, hands-on experiences, and nurturing mentorship— remain just as relevant. They serve as a reminder that education, at its finest's, isn't just about transferring knowledge but about sparking curiosity, fostering critical thinking skills, and shaping well-rounded individuals equipped to navigate life's complexities.

Reflections from Colleagues:

J. Robert Oppenheimer wasn't a figure in the field of physics; he was also highly regarded as a colleague who fostered collaboration and valued intellectual exchange. Those fortunate enough to work alongside him often spoke of the energy he brought to every discussion. Whether it was in his office at the University of California Berkeley or the Institute for Advanced Study in Princeton, Oppenheimer's workspace became a hub for ideas. Scientists, researchers, and scholars frequently gathered there, drawn by Oppenheimer's presence and the promise of thought-provoking conversations.

Oppenheimer approached collaboration with respect for perspectives. Despite being a figure in his field, he never overshadowed the contributions of others. He actively participated in debates with enthusiasm. These discussions would often extend beyond hours as participants got engrossed in the excitement of intellectual exploration.

Dr. Isidor Rabi, a Nobel laureate who worked closely with Oppenheimer, once commented on his humility. Rabi observed that Oppenheimer had a knack for bringing out the best in those around him. He would play devil's advocate not to debunk ideas but to refine and strengthen them.

This approach created an atmosphere where everyone respected each other and grew together. It wasn't about reaching goals but pushing the boundaries of knowledge as a united team.

Another meaningful insight comes from Dr. Hans Bethe, who collaborated with Oppenheimer on projects. He talked about Oppenheimer's unwavering dedication to integrity. In a time when the pursuit of discoveries could sometimes overshadow considerations, Oppenheimer stood as a shining example of clarity. He believed that science in its form was a quest for truth, and this truth should be sought honestly, diligently, and responsibly.

However, despite his brilliance and significant contributions, his compassion made Oppenheimer truly special to his colleagues. Beyond being a genius physicist, he was a caring individual who deeply valued his peers. He rejoiced in their successes, provided support during setbacks, and always made himself available for professional and personal guidance.

In conclusion, while the world admires J. Robert Oppenheimer for his accomplishments, those who knew him intimately cherish their memories of a colleague and friend.
The way they perceive his impact goes beyond being a physicist who altered the path of history. He is remembered as someone who made a difference in the lives of individuals with his compassion, sagacity, and unstoppable determination.

The Enduring Impact of Oppenheimer the Educator:

J. Robert Oppenheimer is widely known for his groundbreaking work as a physicist. His impact as an educator often goes unnoticed amidst his accomplishments. However, those fortunate enough to have been his students or colleagues can attest to Oppenheimer's role as a teacher. His classrooms were not simply places of instruction; they served as arenas for exploration where boundaries of knowledge were constantly pushed and redefined.

Oppenheimer believed education went beyond memorization and dispensing facts; it was about fostering curiosity, nurturing thinking, and instilling a passion for learning. He approached subjects rigorously and relatably, ensuring that even the intricate theories became accessible to his students. His lectures were not one speech; they encouraged questions, sparked debates, and embraced perspectives.

Furthermore, Oppenheimer's dedication to education extended beyond the classroom through mentorship. He took an interest in the development of his students, guiding them not only in their academic pursuits but also in their personal and ethical growth. Inspired by his mentorship, many of his students contributed to science and other fields.

Many attributed their achievements to the years they spent learning from Oppenheimer. Under his guidance, they were encouraged to question, challenge norms and strive for excellence.

However, one of Oppenheimer's lasting legacies as an educator was his belief in the power of education. He viewed teaching as a duty and a responsibility to shape the minds of generations. He often emphasized the vital role educators play in shaping society by instilling values like integrity, empathy, and accountability in their students. Oppenheimer's focus on scientists' moral and social responsibilities was timely and timeless in an era marked by progress and ethical dilemmas.

Upon reflecting on Oppenheimer's life, it becomes apparent that his true greatness extended beyond his contributions to physics; it lay in his ability to inspire thinkers, leaders, and change-makers across generations. His legacy as an educator serves as a reminder of the profound impact teachers can have not on their students but also on society itself.

Oppenheimer's teachings, philosophies, and unyielding dedication to seeking knowledge continue to hold immense significance. They serve as a compass leading us toward a future that's both enlightened and promising.

CHAPTER 8: TRIALS, TRIBULATIONS, AND POLITICS.

J. Robert Oppenheimer's life was marked by many accomplishments, yet it was also overshadowed by political drama and personal challenges. As the 1950s began, the United States was engulfed in a climate of fear and doubt. The Cold War was, in swing, with communism casting a shadow. Oppenheimer was caught up in a whirlwind of accusations, inquiries, and public scrutiny.

The Political Backdrop:

The aftermath of World War II in the United States was not filled with the excitement of victory and was overshadowed by a new kind of conflict known as the Cold War. As the country shifted from a mindset and economy, there was a change in the political climate. The necessary alliance with the Soviet Union to defeat the Axis powers quickly deteriorated into suspicion and rivalry. This shift was driven by the United States and USSR emerging as superpowers armed with capabilities and conflicting ideologies.

The fear of communism, which had been present in America since the Russian Revolution of 1917, became more urgent. The "Red Scare" from the 1920s resurfaced. This time, it was intensified by geopolitical threats posed by the Soviet Union. Events like the establishment of the Iron Curtain in Eastern Europe, the Berlin Blockade, and the successful Soviet nuclear bomb detonation in 1949 all contributed to a sense of unease.

Within U.S. borders, this fear translated into increased scrutiny toward individuals and organizations perceived to be sympathetic to ideologies.

The House Un-American Activities Committee (HUAC), established in 1938, became highly active in investigating allegations of infiltration across sectors of American society. One notable target was Hollywood, given its influence resulting in the blacklisting of numerous artists and professionals.

Senator Joseph McCarthy from Wisconsin fueled communist sentiments by making aggressive and often unfounded accusations against government officials, academics, and other public figures. This period, known as McCarthyism, was characterized by allegations. The use of fear tactics often disregarded proper legal processes. As a result, careers were ruined.

Understanding this context is crucial to grasp the challenges faced by J. Robert Oppenheimer. Oppenheimer found himself at the center of this political storm as a scientist with access to the nation's sensitive nuclear secrets and past affiliations with left-leaning groups. His story encapsulates the tensions of that era—when pursuing security often meant sacrificing liberties and distinguishing between patriotism and dissent became dangerously blurred.

Oppenheimer's Political Leanings:

J. Robert Oppenheimer, despite his accomplishments, had complex political beliefs. During the 1930s, a time overshadowed by the Great Depression in the United States, he held sympathies toward leaning ideologies. Alongside intellectuals and academics of that era, Oppenheimer questioned the existing socio-structures and explored socialist and communist ideas as potential solutions to address the prevailing economic and social challenges.

Oppenheimer's interactions during this period were reflective of a trend among intellectuals. He engaged with groups and attended meetings and events where discussions revolved around socialist and communist concepts. However, it's important to differentiate between association and active membership. Although Oppenheimer associated with individuals aligned with communism, there is no evidence to suggest that he was a member of the Communist Party or held any formal organizational or operational roles. His involvement leaned more toward exploration and philosophical exchanges.

His personal relationships also played a role in shaping perceptions regarding his inclinations. His wife Katherine and brother Frank held views that further fueled speculation about Oppenheimer's beliefs. However, as an intellectual at heart, Oppenheimer often approached ideologies as frameworks for understanding society rather than rigid doctrines to be blindly followed. His political perspectives were adaptable and evolved in response to the changing socio landscape.

The emergence of World War II and the subsequent Cold War impacted Oppenheimer's outlook. As the world grappled with the threat of fascism and, later, the ideological conflict between capitalism and communism, Oppenheimer's focus shifted toward contemplating the implications of nuclear science. His leadership role in the Manhattan Project and firsthand experience witnessing the devastating power of bombs made him acutely aware of the political challenges of the atomic age.

Following World War II, Oppenheimer's political views leaned more toward centrism. While he continued to advocate for cooperation and nuclear disarmament, he distanced himself from leftist ideologies. His reservations about developing hydrogen bombs stemmed from a rooted belief in using advancements responsibly rather than aligning with any particular political group.

In summary, J. Robert Oppenheimer's political leanings blended experiences, intellectual curiosity, and the broader socio-political context during his lifetime.

In the beginning, he was drawn to ideologies. However, as time went on and he experienced the complexities of life during times his perspectives developed and became more sophisticated. This evolution showcased his personality and the challenging era he existed in.

The AEC Hearing:

The 1954 Atomic Energy Commission (AEC) hearing was not a trial for J. Robert Oppenheimer; it represented a significant turning point in the history of science, politics, and post-war America. During the Cold War era characterized by suspicion and paranoia, the hearing became an observed event that captivated the entire nation.

Oppenheimer, who had previously been hailed as the "Father of the Atomic Bomb" and celebrated as a hero for leading the Manhattan Project, found himself in a position. He had to defend his security clearance and unwavering loyalty to the United States. The charges against him were numerous and varied. They included allegations regarding his associations with known communists and accusations surrounding his opposition to developing the hydrogen bomb. However, beneath these specific charges lay a question about scientists' involvement in shaping policies and navigating dissent boundaries during an era of ideological conflicts.

The hearing itself spanned weeks resembling an event. It took place in Washington, D.C., wherein Oppenheimer faced a panel comprising AEC commissioners, legal advisors, and an array of witnesses. The testimonies presented encompassed recollections, scientific discussions, and political interrogations.

Some critical moments occurred when Oppenheimer's former colleagues and friends, such as Edward Teller, took the witness stand. Teller's testimony was particularly perceived as a betrayal by many as he hinted that Oppenheimer might not be trustworthy enough to handle the nation's secrets.

Oppenheimer's testimony demonstrated his ability to express himself eloquently and emotionally. He openly discussed his past, acknowledging his associations but vehemently denying disloyalty. He delved into the challenges brought about by the age expressing his concerns about a nuclear arms race and advocating for international collaboration. Sometimes he was confrontational, questioning the motives of those accusing him. He reflected on the implications of his work and contemplated scientists' responsibilities in the atomic era.

The outcome of the hearing—the withdrawal of Oppenheimer's security clearance—stirred controversy that reverberated throughout the community. Many viewed it as an act driven by revenge—a punishment for Oppenheimer's stance on disarmament. Others saw it as a measure to protect security interests. Regardless of perspectives, the AEC hearing had enduring consequences. It highlighted tensions between science and politics and illuminated risks associated with dissent in an environment. Underscored personal sacrifices resulting from public scrutiny.

The AEC hearing holds a place in history, serving as a reminder of the intricacies that defined the Cold War era. It is proof of the hurdles faced by individuals like Oppenheimer, who were still affected by the ideological conflicts of their time despite their expertise in their fields.

The Verdict and Its Implications:

The revocation of J. Robert Oppenheimer's security clearance by the Atomic Energy Commission was not an administrative action; it carried significant weight and profoundly impacted both the corridors of power and American society. After weeks of scrutiny and deliberation, the verdict proved to be divisive, with some viewing it as a safeguard for national security while others saw it as a politically motivated attempt to silence one of the most outspoken critics of U.S. nuclear policy.

The implications of this decision were far-reaching. On a level, it meant that Oppenheimer's direct involvement in government advisory roles, which he had held with distinction for more than ten years, ended. This decision damaged his reputation, casting doubt on his contributions and raising questions about his loyalty. The emotional and psychological toll on Oppenheimer was evident since he had dedicated years of his life in service to his country, making the verdict feel like an act of betrayal.

Beyond its consequences, this decision also had implications for the scientific community. It conveyed that scientists needed to stay in line or face repercussions. The AECs verdict highlighted the precarious position scientists found themselves in during the Cold War era.

Although their expertise proved invaluable, the ability of these experts to freely express dissenting views and engage in debates became increasingly restricted. The prevailing atmosphere of suspicion and paranoia during that time meant that even the slightest deviation from the stance or any past association could result in punishment, no matter how harmless.

Furthermore, the verdict shed light on the growing divide between the community and the political establishment.

Scientists, known for their commitment to open inquiry and objective truth, often were at odds with politicians who prioritized security and control. The Oppenheimer trial came to represent this tension—a microcosm of the conflicts of that era.

In the following years, various consequences stemming from this verdict were felt. Some scientists grew more cautious and hesitant to express views that could be seen as controversial. Others rallied behind Oppenheimer viewing his trial as an assault on principles such as justice and freedom of expression. Debates regarding scientists' role in policy-making, balancing security and individual rights, and navigating the relationship between sciences and politics continued unabated.

In hindsight, revoking Oppenheimer's security clearance by the AEC can now be seen as a reflection of just how intricate and contradictory the Cold War era was.

During an era marked by scientific progress and significant political changes, the Oppenheimer verdict stands as a reminder of the difficulties and moral quandaries confronting those who bravely navigated the complex intersection of scientific exploration and political dynamics amidst one of the most turbulent times in American history.

The Intersection of Science and Politics:

J. Robert Oppenheimer's journey through mid-20th-century politics highlights the balance between scientific exploration and the ever-changing landscape of political agendas. His challenges were not just battles; they represented the tensions of an era where groundbreaking scientific achievements clashed with political suspicion and Cold War fears. Despite his contributions to the age, Oppenheimer found himself entangled in accusations and distrust, revealing how even highly respected scientists could be affected by geopolitical interests. His story serves as a reminder of the importance of remaining vigilant, transparent, and unwavering in defending freedom, even when faced with immense political pressure. Reflecting on Oppenheimer's trials and tribulations brings to light the struggle to safeguard knowledge from being influenced by term political whims.

THE COURTROOM DRAMA OF THE AEC HEARING:

The 1954 Atomic Energy Commission (AEC) hearing was more than a trial; it was a captivating event that held the nation's attention. Amid all this chaos, J. Robert Oppenheimer found himself at the center, a man once celebrated as a hero but now facing allegations that could tarnish his reputation and revoke his security clearance.

The aftermath of World War II was marked by heightened tensions. The Cold War was in swing. There was an overwhelming fear of communism gripping the United States. This fear, sometimes bordering on paranoia, led to investigations targeting individuals suspected of having ties to communism. The McCarthy hearings had already set a precedent creating an atmosphere of doubt and suspicion.

Setting the Stage:

The United States underwent changes during the mid-20th century. After experiencing the aftermath of World War II, the nation was thrust into a kind of conflict known as the Cold War. This battle between the West and the communist East affected American society. People's minds were filled with pride from victories and anxieties about the uncertainties of age.

During this time, communism loomed large over America, casting a shadow across the country. The Red Scare, as it became known, went beyond politics; it deeply affected people's personal lives. Neighbors began seeing each other suspiciously, and loyalty pledges became commonplace in workplaces. To root out sympathizers of communism, the government launched a series of investigations. Senator Joseph Mccarthy's infamous witch hunts epitomized this era, creating an atmosphere where fear often prevailed over thinking.

Within this context, J. Robert Oppenheimer found himself in a position. As a physicist, he played a role in the Manhattan Project and subsequent atomic bomb development. His contributions had elevated him to national hero status.

However, during the 1950s, the qualities that had once made him highly valued. His intellectual brilliance, perspective, and inclination to question and challenge became sources of controversy.

Oppenheimer's cosmopolitan outlook, connections, and outspoken support for disarmament made him a captivating figure. The nation found itself grappling with its power and the accompanying responsibilities. The atomic era was not about accomplishments; it brought forth deep moral and ethical dilemmas. Oppenheimer symbolized these challenges with his ability to navigate between the realms of science, philosophy, and politics.

As murmurs and speculations regarding his loyalty began to circulate, the stage was set for one of the trials of that era. The 1954 Atomic Energy Commission (AEC) hearings aimed not to determine Oppenheimer's allegiance but also reflected a nation in introspection. The trial delved into the core of identity while questioning the balance between security and freedom or individual rights versus collective well-being.

In this charged atmosphere, the AEC hearing went beyond being a legal proceeding; it became a captivating spectacle where the larger societal debates of that era unfolded. It held the nation's attention; left a mark in history that would be remembered by future generations.

The Charges and the Atmosphere:

The atmosphere in the hearing room of the Atomic Energy Commission was tense, reflecting the sentiment across the nation. During the 1950s, America was gripped by an unease caused by the Cold War, which impacted every aspect of society. The fear of communism was not merely a stance; it permeated life for many people. This environment of suspicion and distrust was further fueled by Senator Joseph Mccarthy's campaigns against those he perceived as sympathetic to communism. The McCarthy hearings set a precedent where anyone, regardless of status or contributions, could suddenly face scrutiny.

Against this backdrop, J. Robert Oppenheimer's hearing commenced with charges laid against him. At its core was the question of loyalty; Could Oppenheimer be trusted with the nation's secrets, given his previous associations and outspoken views? The prosecution presented a list of accusations to cast doubt on his allegiance to the United States. They highlighted his connections from the 1930s when Oppenheimer had affiliations with individuals associated with the Communist Party. Per the prosecution's perspective, these associations served as evidence of conflicts of interest or betrayal.

However, it wasn't about affiliations. Oppenheimer's position on issues and his stance on nuclear disarmament added an extra layer of complexity. During a time when the atomic bomb was seen as a deterrent against aggression, any opposition to its development or deployment was met with suspicion. Oppenheimer's concerns about the hydrogen bomb, particularly, were portrayed as being out of touch with the nation's security needs.

The hearing room transformed into a stage for drama. Each testimony and piece of evidence was carefully deliberated upon by the commission and the general public. The media provided updates through newspapers and radio broadcasts, each offering their interpretation of the proceedings. The nation became divided in its views. Oppenheimer was a hero to some—a scientist dedicated to his country. To others, he was seen as a traitor caught between conflicting loyalties to his ideology and his nation.

As days turned into weeks, the weight of the accusations and the suffocating atmosphere began to take its toll. The hearing ceased to be a process; it reflected society's fears, biases, and internal conflicts.

The Defense Rises:

As the AEC hearing began, all eyes in the nation were fixed on the courtroom. Oppenheimer remained composed and approached the proceedings with a demeanor showing his true scientific nature. His defense went beyond refuting the charges against him; it was about reaffirming his loyalty to his country and his unwavering commitment to expanding knowledge.

From the start, it was clear that Oppenheimer's defense would be grounded in his accomplishments and contributions. The Manhattan Project, which ended World War II, was evidence of his leadership skills and scientific expertise. Those who had worked closely with him during those years quickly came to his support. They depicted a man passionate about his work, driven by a sense of duty and guided by an unyielding compass, always striving for the greater good.

Testimonies from witnesses played a role in presenting Oppenheimer as an individual. Former students remembered his captivating lectures and how he could simplify ideas effortlessly while showing interest in their academic growth. Colleagues from institutions like UC Berkeley and Caltech spoke highly of his spirit, insatiable intellectual curiosity, and unwavering ethical principles, even when faced with difficult choices.

One of the moments during the defense argument was when they recalled Oppenheimer's immediate reaction after the successful test of the first atomic bomb in New Mexico. Oppenheimer's quotation from the Bhagavad Gita, "Now I am become Death, the destroyer of worlds," showcased his knowledge and provided a glimpse into his inner turmoil regarding creating such a devastating weapon.

However, the defense also acknowledged Oppenheimer's associations during his younger years. They argued that, like intellectuals in the 1930s, he explored political ideologies, but that didn't imply disloyalty. They suggested that his ability to question, debate, and evolve his views demonstrated freedom—a quality of admiration instead of condemnation.

As the defense presented its case, it painted a picture of an individual. Oppenheimer was not a physicist but also a mentor, collaborator, leader, and, above all else—a patriot. They argued that his life's work had an unwavering dedication to his country even when he grappled with dilemmas arising from his scientific breakthroughs.

The defense aimed to bring to light the essence of J. Robert Oppenheimer going beyond what was portrayed in the media and political circles. They highlighted his side, contributions, and unwavering commitment to improving society.

The Accusations:

The prosecution had a multifaceted case against Oppenheimer, aiming to portray him as someone whose loyalties were divided or even antagonistic toward the United States. They focused on Oppenheimer's past and connections during the 1930s, a decade marked by hardships and the emergence of different political ideologies.

During the Great Depression, many intellectuals, artists, and scientists were attracted to communism as they saw it as a solution to the economic difficulties of that time. Oppenheimer was among them. The prosecution presented his associations with members of the Communist Party, including his brother Frank and his fiancée Jean Tatlock as evidence of his alleged sympathies. They argued that these associations were indiscretions indicative of an ideological alignment.

They delved into incidents and conversations from Oppenheimer's past. One such incident involved a discussion with Haakon Chevalier, a friend and professor at the University of California in Berkeley. The conversation centered around the possibility of sharing secrets with the Soviet Union. The prosecution portrayed this conversation in a manner suggesting Oppenheimer had knowledge or involvement in discussions about espionage.

It wasn't his connections that came under scrutiny. Oppenheimer's professional judgments, including his opposition to projects and recommendations for positions, were closely examined and presented as evidence of his questionable reliability. The fact that he had access to information only intensified the stakes.

The prosecution's plan was clear; to plant seeds of uncertainty about Oppenheimer's character and intentions. They aimed to depict him with a history of decisions, associations, and choices motivated by personal beliefs rather than national interests.

In Cold War politics, where appearances often held more weight than facts, the accusations against Oppenheimer were powerful. They capitalized on the era's fears and suspicions, transforming one of the nation's intellectuals into a figure shrouded in controversy and uncertainty.

The Hydrogen Bomb Controversy:

Throughout the pages of political history, a few subjects have sparked much controversy, such as the development of the hydrogen bomb. The devastating impact of weapons was already demonstrated by the bombings of Hiroshima and Nagasaki. Still, the hydrogen bomb, known as the "super," represented a significant leap in destructive power. Its potential yield, measured in megatons of kilotons, rendered it a powerful weapon.

J. Robert Oppenheimer, who played a role in developing the bomb, found himself at the center of debates surrounding the hydrogen bomb. His reservations about this project stemmed from ethical and geopolitical concerns. From a standpoint creating a thermonuclear weapon posed challenges. It wasn't simply an extension of bombs; it required new approaches and breakthroughs.

However, Oppenheimer's concerns reached beyond science. The ethical implications weighed heavily on him when considering the creation of such a weapon. The atomic bomb had already ushered in an era of warfare. With the hydrogen bomb on the horizon, there was potential for an unprecedented escalation in an arms race. Oppenheimer questioned whether it was morally justifiable to develop a weapon of obliterating cities or potentially even civilizations.

From a perspective, the situation was extremely critical. The Cold War was. There was a standoff between the United States and the Soviet Union. While some argued that it was crucial to develop the hydrogen bomb to maintain an advantage, Oppenheimer held a view. He believed that its existence could destabilize a balance of power. Oppenheimer feared that pursuing the hydrogen bomb might trigger an arms race, potentially leading to a conflict.

Oppenheimer's stance on the hydrogen bomb created conflicts within the community and political circles. While some praised him for taking a stand, others were suspicious of his loyalty. They questioned his motives. The debate surrounding the hydrogen bomb went beyond discussing the weapon itself; it became a test of loyalty, patriotism, and one's position on the dynamics of the Cold War.

Despite Oppenheimer's concerns, the United States developed and successfully tested the hydrogen bomb in 1952. This marked a phase in the age with an imminent threat of thermonuclear warfare hanging over humanity. Oppenheimer's reservations may not have been heeded at that time. They shed light on moral and ethical dilemmas faced by scientists during this atomic era.

With a reflective tone, he expressed a contrasting perspective amidst the prevailing winds of the era. His words served as a reminder to the world about the responsibilities that accompany power.

The Verdict and Its Implications:

The resounding sound of the gavel in the AEC hearing reverberated beyond the courtroom walls. The revocation of J. Robert Oppenheimer's security clearance carried more weight than an administrative decision; it symbolized a significant shift in American politics and highlighted the vulnerable position of scientists in the atomic age. Oppenheimer, once esteemed as the "Father of the Atomic Bomb," now found himself abruptly excluded from circles.

The verdict was a result of dynamics at play. At its core, it represented a balance between security and individual rights. The Cold War era fostered an overarching mentality that pitted "us versus them." In such an environment, any deviation from the established narrative or even a hint of dissent was met with suspicion. Oppenheimer's vocal opposition to the hydrogen bomb and his past associations, regardless of their remoteness or tenuousness, cast doubt on his loyalty. Stripping him of his clearance served not as a message to Oppenheimer but as a warning to other scientists. It starkly reminded them that there was tolerance for opposing viewpoints in this high-stakes game of politics.

However, it is important to recognize that this verdict had reaching implications beyond its consequences.

It ignited a discussion about the involvement of scientists in policymaking. Should scientists, who understand the intricacies and implications of their work, have a say in how their discoveries are utilized? Or should they be limited to being technicians creating tools for policymakers to utilize as they, please? The AEC hearing brought these questions to the forefront compelling the nation to grapple with the moral aspects of exploration.

The trial emphasized the relationship between science and politics. Although distinct, these two domains are interconnected. The Manhattan Project demonstrated what can be accomplished when science and politics collaborate harmoniously. However, the AEC hearing shed light on the challenges in this relationship. When political considerations overshadow judgment, outcomes can become both unpredictable and far-reaching.

The scientific community found itself at a junction in the aftermath of the verdict. The trial served as a wake-up call that spurred introspection and debate. For individuals, it underscored scientists' need to voice their opinions passionately. They advocated for the responsible use of their discoveries while ensuring that science remains free from undue political influence.

Ultimately the outcome of Oppenheimer's trial went beyond assessing an individual's allegiance. It symbolized the prevailing sentiments and hopes of the era, gauging the nation's concerns and ambitions. It stood as a reminder of the complexities and obligations that accompany harnessing breakthroughs during times of political instability.

Reflections on the Hearing:

The AEC hearing concerning J. Robert Oppenheimer was more than an event; it represented that time's wider societal and political tensions. As the gavel struck and testimonies reverberated in the courtroom, the trial encapsulated the battles of the Cold War. It questioned what it truly meant to be a loyal American and a scientist.

Oppenheimer's trial mirrored an era where personal beliefs and national loyalty often intertwined. The hearing served as a manifestation of society's anxieties at that moment. The specter of communism, the scars left by world wars, and leaps forward in science fostered an atmosphere filled with suspicion and fear. In such an environment, individuals like Oppenheimer. With their nuanced perspectives and complex personalities. Became targets for those who sought narratives pitting good against evil.

Additionally, this hearing highlighted the balance between exploration and national security. Science is driven by a quest for knowledge that transcends borders or allegiances; it is a pursuit. However, in geopolitics, where knowledge translates into power, science can become a tool or weapon.

Oppenheimer's trial brought attention to this contrast raising inquiries about the involvement of scientists in shaping policies and the degree to which their work should be influenced by factors.

The personal toll on Oppenheimer was evident. Its repercussions extended beyond him. The scientific community observed with unease realizing that the integrity of their work was not immune to maneuvering. Young scientists who admired Oppenheimer as a guiding light were left disenchanted, questioning their role in a world where intellectual curiosity could be misunderstood as disloyalty.

Looking back at the AEC hearing now serves as a reminder of the intricacies of that era. It prompts us to ponder the concept of loyalty, the responsibilities of geniuses, and the cost of expressing dissent. As we retrospectively examine these events, we are compelled to ask; In our pursuit of security, did we compromise the principles we aimed to safeguard?

The Legacy of the AEC Hearing:

The AEC hearing, which examined J. Robert Oppenheimer extensively, was not an incident in history. Instead, it symbolized an era characterized by ideologies, political maneuvering, and the turbulent relationship between science and politics. The impact of this trial extended beyond the courtroom, influencing the community at large policy-making processes and the collective mindset of our nation.

Oppenheimer's trial revealed how vulnerable one's reputation can be when political expediency comes into play. A man once celebrated as a hero for his role in ushering in the atomic age found himself marginalized when his views diverged from the prevailing sentiments of that time. This transition from admiration to suspicion light on the challenges faced by those who dared to express dissent or question the status quo during heightened national tension.

This hearing served as a reminder of the dilemmas inherent in scientific exploration. As known as the "Father of the Atomic Bomb," Oppenheimer grappled with the implications of his work—a struggle that became public during this trial. His vocal opposition to hydrogen bombs and his advocacy for disarmament were not merely beliefs but also represented broader debates within the scientific community regarding their responsibilities when making groundbreaking discoveries.

The AEC hearing had lasting effects on the relationship between scientists and policymakers. The trial's outcome, the decision to revoke Oppenheimer's security clearance, sent a message to the scientific community; conform or face consequences. This situation, where political considerations could overshadow expertise, had implications for policymaking and the role of scientists in shaping it.

When contemplating the legacy of the AEC hearing, one cannot. Think about the complexities of Oppenheimer's life and his era. His story, intertwined with the narrative of the Cold War, serves as a testament to the challenges that arise at the intersection of science, ethics, and politics – both on a level and within society. As we look ahead, we should remember the lessons from this trial that are still relevant today. They remind us to strike a balance between rights, scientific exploration, and national interests.

CHAPTER 9: THE GLOBAL ATOMIC STAGE.

The explosion of the bomb in 1945 not only represented a remarkable scientific accomplishment but also signaled the commencement of a fresh era in worldwide politics and diplomacy. The atomic age, led by J. Robert Oppenheimer, completely transformed the scenario bringing about a fundamental change in power dynamics and international relations.

The Birth of the Nuclear Age:

The explosion of the bomb in 1945 went beyond being the culmination of years of extensive scientific research. It marked the beginning of an era in history. Up until then, wars had been fought using weapons. Now the world was introduced to an unmatched force of destruction. The towering mushroom cloud that emerged over the deserts of New Mexico during the Trinity test represented the changes about to unfold. It served as a symbol of humanity's ability to harness nature's fundamental forces, although with both awe-inspiring and terrifying consequences.

In the aftermath of the Trinity test, emotions ran high with a mix of excitement and contemplation. Scientists like Oppenheimer, who were involved in this project, witnessing a detonation, validated their work, theories, and calculations. However, this achievement also brought along a sense of responsibility. The sheer power demonstrated by the bomb made it clear that warfare would never be the same again. The bombings in Hiroshima and Nagasaki further emphasized this reality. In moments two cities were reduced to ruins. Tens of thousands lost their lives.

The devastating images, survivor accounts, and long-term consequences of radiation brought to light the moral considerations surrounding the use of such a weapon.

The global community, already grappling with the horrors of World War II, was confronted with a challenge. The atomic bomb was not a weapon; it completely altered the landscape of diplomacy, strategy, and geopolitics. Nations began to realize that possessing this weapon meant holding power not on the battlefield but also in diplomatic negotiations. This marked the dawn of the age, accompanied by challenges ranging from proliferation concerns to arms control issues and Cold War dynamics between superpowers.

For Oppenheimer and his contemporaries, this epoch marked a moment for introspection. Scientists once confined to laboratories found themselves amid discussions on ethics, policy-making, and international relations. The boundaries between science, politics, and morality became increasingly indistinct. The question shifted from whether humanity could create such a weapon to whether it should. In essence, the age's birth represented a juncture in human history.

During an era marked by progress, deep contemplation emerged regarding humanity's role in the cosmos and our obligations to future generations. The atomic bomb, with its might and capacity for devastation, epitomized the complexities and moral quandaries of the century.

The Proliferation Dilemma:

The introduction of the bomb in 1945 brought a level of power to the world, something that was previously only seen in nature's most devastating events. However, this remarkable achievement came with challenges. One of the challenges was the issue of proliferation, which involved a complex network of political, ethical, and security concerns relating to the potential spread of nuclear weapons.

After World War II, the United States had nuclear capabilities. This exclusivity didn't last long. The allure of weapons and their promise of military superiority proved irresistible to many countries, especially those with aspirations for global influence. The Soviet Union recognized the advantage held by the U.S., expedited its nuclear program, and successfully tested its first atomic bomb in 1949. This not only heightened tensions during the Cold War but also marked the beginning of an arms race that would shape politics for decades.

The rapid progress made by superpowers in developing weapons raised concerns worldwide. It wasn't about the United States and the USSR; there was a growing realization that other nations driven by conflicts or global ambitions would also strive for such weaponry. The potential widespread distribution of arms posed threats. On the one hand, there were worries about security.

The increase in nations possessing capabilities posed a risk of nuclear conflict, whether intentional or accidental. However, there were concerns to consider. The bombings of Hiroshima and Nagasaki vividly demonstrated the devastating consequences of warfare. The idea that multiple countries could possess power raised moral questions about the future of humanity itself.

Oppenheimer, who played a role in the age's birth, was keenly aware of these challenges. After World War II, he transformed from being a physicist to an advocate for nuclear control. He envisioned a world where atomic energy would be utilized for purposes than destruction. However, his calls for cooperation and control often faced skepticism and resistance during the Cold War era.

The proliferation dilemma also prompted efforts as nations negotiated treaties and agreements to curb the spread of weapons. While these endeavors had varying levels of success, they highlighted a consensus on preventing an arms race in terms of nuclear weaponry.

Ultimately the proliferation dilemma was not a challenge; it reflected broader concerns within the atomic age.

It illuminated the contradiction within human advancement, where scientific progress while expanding the limits of what's achievable also raised ethical and existential inquiries.

The Balance of Terror:

The "Balance of Terror" concept emerged during the Cold War, representing the equilibrium between the superpowers of that time, the United States and the Soviet Union. The foundation of this balance lay in the doctrine called Mutually Assured Destruction (MAD), an idea that suggested neither superpower would launch an attack first as they knew that the other side would retaliate with equal or greater force resulting in both nations being completely destroyed. This mutual vulnerability created a situation where weapons sheer destructive power acted as a deterrent against their use.

Both superpowers further heightened this equilibrium by developing and stockpiling missiles (ICBMs), submarine-launched ballistic missiles (SLBMs), and long-range bombers. These delivery systems ensured that even if one nation's land-based missiles were destroyed in a strike, submarines or airborne bombers would still exist to launch a devastating counterattack. This trio of nuclear delivery systems reinforced MADs concept by making the consequences of warfare too catastrophic for either side to bear. However, despite this balance, there were moments when fragility prevailed. Events like the Cuban Missile Crisis in 1962 brought the world close to a conflict.

The entire world was captivated for thirteen days as the United States and the Soviet Union found themselves in a stakes diplomatic standoff with nuclear warheads positioned just minutes away from their intended targets. During this time, the true realization of the consequences that could arise from a nuclear exchange emerged, ultimately leading to a peaceful resolution of the crisis. These events served as a reminder of the risks associated with what was known as the Balance of Terror. A delicate equilibrium where any miscalculations or misinterpretations could inadvertently ignite a catastrophic nuclear conflict.

While the doctrine of Assured Destruction (MAD) provided some semblance of stability, it also sparked debates and introspection regarding the morality and ethics behind relying on the threat of total destruction to maintain peace. Intellectuals, policymakers, and ordinary citizens alike grappled with questions about living under the fear of nuclear obliteration. One notable figure in this discourse was J. Robert Oppenheimer, who famously referenced scripture by quoting from the Bhagavad Gita; "Now I am become Death, the destroyer of worlds." This quote encapsulates the dilemmas faced by humanity in an era where we possess unimaginable power to destroy ourselves.

In retrospect, within humanity's trajectory, the Balance of Terror is an enduring testament to our complex nature. On the one hand, it showcased our technological achievements; on the other hand, it laid bare before us the immense challenges associated with wielding such tremendous power responsibly.

In this era, where tensions exist, but major conflicts between superpowers are absent, it is a reminder of how power, responsibility, and survival intertwine in the nuclear age.

Oppenheimer's Role on the Global Stage:

J. Robert Oppenheimer gained recognition as the "Father of the Atomic Bomb," which naturally placed him in the spotlight and made him a key figure in the debates and conversations that shaped the era following World War II. Although his direct involvement in policymaking decreased after the Manhattan Project, his influence on discussions surrounding weapons and atomic energy was profound.

In the aftermath of World War II, Oppenheimer's expertise was highly sought after by policymakers and international organizations. He actively advocated for using energy for purposes and called for international control over atomic weapons. He firmly believed that if not properly regulated, the immense power of atoms could result in consequences. Oppenheimer consistently emphasized the importance of an approach to utilizing atomic energy for humanity's benefit instead of its destruction.

Oppenheimer engaged with scientists, diplomats, and leaders worldwide through his participation in conferences and symposiums. These interactions went beyond discussions; they delved into ethical considerations regarding nuclear weapons. With his eloquence and profound understanding of the subject matter, Oppenheimer became a voice in these forums. He advocated for a world where nations collaborated on research, shared knowledge openly, and worked toward disarmament.

However, there were some controversies surrounding his perspectives. Given the rivalry between the U.S. and the USSR during the Cold War, Oppenheimer's calls for collaboration and disarmament were often met with suspicion. His previous affiliations and outspoken opinions caused tensions with military authorities resulting in the withdrawal of his security clearance in

1954. Though this incident was a setback for Oppenheimer, it shed light on the challenges faced by scientists in an era dominated by technology, where their work had political and societal implications.

Nevertheless, Oppenheimer's influence endured despite these obstacles. He continued to shape discussions on energy and weaponry through his lectures, writings, and public involvement. He became a symbol of scientists' moral responsibility during the age, consistently reminding the world of the quandaries presented by nuclear weapons. His lasting impact shows how reasoned debates, exploration, and ethical contemplation can shape historical trajectories.

The Test Ban Treaties:

The Test Ban Treaties, the Partial Test Ban Treaty (PTBT) of 1963 marked a turning point in the history of nuclear diplomacy. During the 1950s and early 1960s, major powers, like the United States and the Soviet Union, conducted a series of tests. These tests, which often had power and impact, not displayed their nuclear capabilities but also raised widespread concerns about radioactive fallout and its potential global effects.

The international community was already dealing with tensions during the Cold War when they faced a challenge; understanding the environmental and health consequences of atmospheric nuclear tests. Reports started emerging about regions from test sites being affected by contamination. People became increasingly worried about how these tests would affect health, agriculture, and the environment in the run. It wasn't the public who expressed concern; even scientists involved in developing nuclear weapons began expressing their worries.

Considering this context, discussions were initiated to explore a treaty that could ban testing altogether. The negotiations faced challenges due to mistrust between powers, concerns regarding verification methods, and conflicting national interests; reaching an agreement proved to be a journey.

However, nations shared an understanding of the catastrophe that ongoing testing could unleash, which created a common ground.

These efforts culminated in the signing of the Partial Test Ban Treaty in 1963. This treaty, endorsed by the United States, the Soviet Union, and the United Kingdom, strictly prohibited tests in the atmosphere, underwater and outer space. While it didn't include tests in its ban, the PTBT marked an initial step toward achieving nuclear disarmament. Its significance extended beyond its provisions; it also conveyed a message that major world powers could come together to address shared challenges.

J. Robert Oppenheimer's advocacy for disarmament and arms control had long emphasized the ethical dilemmas associated with atomic weapons. Although he wasn't directly involved in negotiating this treaty, his vision of a world where atomic energy was utilized for purposes resonated strongly with the ideals embodied by PTBT.

Over the years, PTBT paved the way for inclusive arms control agreements such as the Non-Proliferation Treaty (NPT) and Comprehensive Test Ban Treaty (CTBT). Although there are still obstacles to overcome, the Test Ban Treaties stand as evidence of how countries worldwide can unite when faced with dangers.

The path leading to the Test Ban Treaties was filled with discoveries, political strategies, and moral discussions, providing a glimpse into the complexities and possibilities of the atomic era. It highlights the equilibrium between priorities and global obligations, between striving for dominance and a safer, fairer world.

The Legacy of the Atomic Age:

The era of power, which began with the detonation of the nuclear bomb, left an enduring impact on human history. Its influence extended beyond science and technology, shaping geopolitics, culture, and the collective consciousness of societies.

The immediate aftermath of the bombings in Hiroshima and Nagasaki brought the force of nuclear weapons into sharp focus. The world witnessed devastation, sparking debates about the ethical implications of possessing such power. Even scientists like Oppenheimer grappled with their responsibility for creating weapons. This self-reflection triggered discussions on how science should be used in society, with many scientists advocating for applications of atomic energy and promoting disarmament.

As the Cold War escalated, both superpowers amassed arsenals resulting in an era marked by a delicate balance of power. The concept known as Assured Destruction (MAD) emerged during this time. It suggested that a scale nuclear conflict between these superpowers would lead to destruction. While this paradoxically maintained peace, it also highlighted security vulnerability.

The Cuban Missile Crisis in 1962 symbolized this tension pushing the world close to war and emphasizing the urgent need for diplomacy and disarmament.

During this time of the century, there were concerted efforts to control the spread of nuclear weapons. Treaties like the Non-Proliferation Treaty (NPT) aimed to prevent weapon proliferation and encourage disarmament. Although often challenging, these global agreements represented a recognition of the risks associated with nuclear proliferation.

In terms of culture, the age influenced art, literature, and cinema as they reflected society's fears, aspirations, and profound questions regarding existence in an era dominated by nuclear power. The atomic age greatly impacted creative expression, from stories envisioning apocalyptic worlds to philosophical works exploring power dynamics and responsibility.

Looking back, the legacy of the age serves as a reminder of both the positive and negative aspects of scientific discovery. While this era brought advancements in energy production, medicine, and various scientific fields, it also presented challenges that tested humanity's wisdom and diplomatic capabilities. The lessons from this period emphasize the significance of considerations in endeavors and our shared responsibility to use knowledge wisely with foresight and prudence.

Navigating the Atomic Crossroads:

The era of power, which scientists like J. Robert Oppenheimer initiated, presented humanity with both opportunities and challenges. On the one hand, it held the promise of energy and the potential to transform industries offering hope for a future powered by energy. On the hand, there was the looming threat of destruction, ethical dilemmas surrounding such immense power, and the delicate diplomatic balancing acts that nations had to navigate for many years.

Oppenheimer's journey during this period reflects the narrative. A man of intellect and introspection, he grappled with the consequences of his work. Represented the complex issues faced by the world. His transformation from leading the Manhattan Project to becoming an advocate for disarmament and peace highlights the nature of living in an age.

As we contemplate this chapter in history, it becomes clear that the global stage dominated by power was not about political dynamics or scientific accomplishments. At its core, it delved into aspects of nature—our ability to create and destroy—and examined the choices we confront when standing at critical junctures in history.

Oppenheimer's impact, closely connected to the story of the era, stands as a reminder of the immense weight of responsibility and our everlasting pursuit, of peaceful coexistence, in a nuclear-powered world.

INTERACTIVE MAPS AND OPPENHEIMER'S GLOBAL INFLUENCE:

The era of power, which began with the explosion of the atomic bomb in 1945, was not limited to America alone. Its effects rippled worldwide, reshaping politics and leaving a lasting mark on history. At the center of this period stood J. Robert Oppenheimer, whose influence extended beyond Los Alamos or even the borders of the United States. To truly comprehend Oppenheimer's impact on a scale, one must embark on a journey across continents, exploring the intricate international relations, scientific collaborations, and political intrigues that characterized the mid-20th century.

The European Response: A Continent Divided:

After World War II, Europe experienced changes; the wounds of the war were still fresh cities lay in ruins. There were shifts in the political landscape of the continent. The introduction of the bomb added a layer of complexity to this volatile situation. Europe, known for its history of exploration and discoveries, had to face the reality that atomic power was no longer just a concept but a powerful force.

J. Robert Oppenheimer played a role as one of the figures in shaping the atomic age, and he became an important topic of discussion among European scientists and politicians. Within the community, there was both awe and admiration for the brilliance displayed by Oppenheimer's Manhattan Project and its rapid advancements. Many European physicists who had fled from fascism in their home countries had collaborated with Oppenheimer in America and now pondered over the implications of their collective achievements.

Politically the bomb had consequences as it marked the beginning of the Cold War, with Europe becoming its battleground. The continent was effectively divided into Eastern and Western blocs, with a separation symbolized by the Iron Curtain.

The atomic bomb quickly became a symbol of power playing a role in high-stakes international diplomacy. While Oppenheimer's work was lauded in the world, it faced scrutiny from the East. The Soviet Union, driven by its desire to establish its capabilities, saw the Manhattan Project as both a challenge and an opportunity. This led to heightened espionage efforts, with spies dispatched to extract information from research facilities like Los Alamos.

However, beyond the realm of politics and science, there was a response. The people of Europe, who had already endured the horrors of two devastating world wars, viewed the bomb with fear and resignation. The bombings of Hiroshima and Nagasaki served as reminders of humanity's potential through its inventions—Oppenheimer's famous reflection on the Bhagavad Gita. "Now I am become Death, the destroyer of worlds" struck a chord within a continent that had witnessed destruction.

In circles spanning across cafes and salons, passionate debates arose regarding science's role in society. Philosophers, writers, and artists grappled with questions from the atomic age. Oppenheimer himself became a symbol of the scientist and philosopher. Someone who encapsulated the complexities of those times. Thanks to his profound appreciation for literature and philosophy.

Europe's reaction to Oppenheimer and the atomic era can be complex and varied. It encompassed a mixture of admiration, introspection, fear, and hope. The continent, with its history, culture, and intellectual heritage, had to redefine its position in a world where the power of nuclear energy had permanently altered.

Asia and the Shadow of Hiroshima and Nagasaki:

The nuclear bombings in Hiroshima and Nagasaki in August 1945 did not mark the end of World War II—they also symbolized the beginning of a new era in global geopolitics, with Asia at the center of it all. The immediate devastation caused by these bombs served as a reminder of how destructive nuclear energy can be. Entire cities were completely destroyed, and countless lives were lost within moments. However, the aftermath was not limited to those moments; survivors, known as "hibakusha," had to confront the long-term effects of radiation exposure on their mental well-being.

Beyond the tragedy, these bombings had far-reaching implications for Asia as a whole. Already grappling with the aftermath of a prolonged war, Japan was forced into a period of introspection and reconstruction. The nation faced the challenges of rebuilding its cities while also addressing the trauma experienced by its citizens. The atomic bombings became a part of Japan's memory, influencing its subsequent commitment to pacifism and nuclear disarmament in the post-war era. Oppenheimer is regarded as one of the figures behind these bombs' scientific development, seen through a lens encompassing respect, resentment, and curiosity. His subsequent contemplations on the implications tied to his work resonated strongly with a nation seeking answers and solace. The impact of Hiroshima and Nagasaki extended beyond Japan's borders.

In China, a country that suffered greatly from aggression, during the war, the bombings were viewed as a means of liberation and retribution. However, as the dynamics of the Cold War emerged, China's perspective shifted. Pursuing capability became a symbol of pride and security, with Oppenheimer's research serving as both inspiration and a warning.

India, on the verge of gaining independence from colonial rule, was also deeply impacted by the events of 1945. Leaders like Jawaharlal Nehru, who later became India's Prime Minister, openly condemned the bombings. Nehru envisioned an India based on non-violence and peaceful coexistence. The atomic era brought strategic dilemmas due to its potential for destruction. Oppenheimer's subsequent advocacy for disarmament and his contemplation on the aspects of scientific discovery resonated within India's policy circles. His interactions with scientists and policymakers, including a visit to the country in the 1950s, further strengthened their engagement.

Southeast Asia countries such as Indonesia, Vietnam, and the Philippines may not have been directly involved in the race but closely observed shifting power dynamics.

The atomic bomb, with its potential, for power, symbolized the challenges and opportunities faced by the colonial world. Oppenheimer's work combined scientific. Ethical contemplation makes it a focal point for discussions on how science contributes to nation-building and the responsibilities accompanying progress.

In essence, the events in Hiroshima and Nagasaki cast a shadow over Asia, shaping the scientific and moral landscapes of the continent. J. Robert Oppenheimer played a role in this narrative as a figure influencing policy decisions guiding scientific endeavors and sparking philosophical debates that continue to have an impact even today.

The Middle East: Oil, Politics, and the Atomic Equation:

The Middle East, a region with a history of cultures, religions, and empires, found itself at the intersection of modern geopolitics and the emerging atomic age. Given its oil reserves hidden beneath its landscapes, the region had already been a focal point in global power dynamics. The discovery and subsequent utilization of energy added another layer to the political landscape of the Middle East.

The significance of Oil as the lifeblood of economies firmly established the Middle East as an area of strategic importance. Nations like Saudi Arabia, boasting oil fields, became players in global politics. The intertwining of oil politics with the power potential presented opportunities and challenges. Countries within the region began recognizing that atomic energy held potential; as a catalyst for development and progress and a potent weapon capable of reshaping regional power dynamics.

The work conducted by J. Robert Oppenheimer on developing bombs and his advocacy for nuclear disarmament resonated deeply within the Middle East. While immediate concerns in the region revolved around disputes and nation-building efforts, its leaders were not oblivious to the implications of living in a world with nuclear weapons.

Countries like Israel, located in a region with neighbors, had to carefully consider the strategic and ethical implications of pursuing nuclear capabilities. The secretive nature of programs in the area, combined with the political environment, made the Middle East a potential hotspot when it came to global nuclear dynamics.

Iran, a nation with a history and aspirations for influence, saw atomic energy as a way to assert its position on the world stage. However, its endeavors to harness power for purposes were often met with suspicion by the international community. This led to efforts involving negotiations and sanctions. Even as Iran sought its path toward utilizing energy, there were echoes of Oppenheimer's emphasis on international control and peaceful utilization resonating within Tehran's diplomatic circles.

The Middle East's intricate relationship with Cold War superpowers. The United States and the Soviet Union. Added layers of complexity to the atomic equation. Both superpowers recognized the importance of this region. They used promises of nuclear technology as leverage to extend their influence. When considering factors such as oil politics, Cold War dynamics, and advancements in energy during that era, it becomes clear that the Middle East held significance within the global discourse surrounding nuclear power.

Essentially the experience of the Middle East during the age reflected its blend of history, culture, and politics. The prospect of energy, with its possibilities for progress and deterrence, was carefully evaluated alongside the strategic and political hurdles it posed. Throughout this period, the contributions and beliefs of J. Robert Oppenheimer stood as a guiding light shedding light on both the benefits and dangers of the era.

Africa and Latin America: The Quest for Atomic Autonomy:

After the end of World War II, when the world was grappling with the impact of the age, Africa and Latin America found themselves at a crucial turning point. These regions, known for their history and vibrant cultures, emerged from the era of colonialism and foreign control. They were determined to shape their destinies in a changing global landscape.

For nations, the middle of the 20th century marked a time of political awakening and a strong drive for independence. The atomic age brought both opportunities and challenges. On the one hand, nuclear technology holds the potential for progress in sectors like energy, medicine, and agriculture. Utilizing energy for purposes could accelerate growth, reduce reliance on traditional energy sources and pave the way for a brighter future. However, there were also concerns about how nuclear weapons could affect geopolitics as superpowers engaged in an arms race. African nations aimed to avoid being used as pawns in this high-stakes game while prioritizing their interests and autonomy.

Latin America faced dilemmas during this period of advancement due to its diverse mix of cultures and histories.

Countries like Brazil and Argentina, driven by their growing economies and aspirations for prominence, saw technology as a way to assert their global presence. The scientific communities in these nations were eager to collaborate, learn, and contribute to the expanding research frontiers. However, the Cold War cast a shadow over this endeavor. The ideological rivalry between the United States and the Soviet Union had echoes in Latin America, with countries being courted, coerced, or pressured to align with one bloc. Pursuing autonomy became intertwined with broader struggles for sovereignty, non-alignment, and regional solidarity in this context.

J. Robert Oppenheimer's legacy extends beyond his association with the Manhattan Project and the creation of the bomb; it also had influences on these regions. His advocacy for the uses of energy, his cautious stance on nuclear proliferation, and his nuanced understanding of the ethical dimensions of scientific exploration resonated with leaders and intellectuals in Africa and Latin America. They perceived Oppenheimer as a scientist who recognized the responsibility that accompanies groundbreaking innovation.

It was not just about harnessing atomic power for Africa and Latin America during the age. It represented their dreams, difficulties, and the determined quest, for independence, in a changing world. The story of these areas spoke volumes about their strength, foresight, and unwavering determination to shape their destiny in the records of the time.

The Global Scientific Community: Collaborations and Confrontations:

The era of the age brought about groundbreaking discoveries that had significant implications. It also led to a time of collaboration and occasional clashes. As countries grappled with the realities of power, the global scientific community found itself at a junction where knowledge, ethics, and geopolitics intersected.

Amidst this milieu, J. Robert Oppenheimer emerged as a central figure due to his unparalleled expertise and leadership in developing the atomic bomb. While his work was rooted in the challenges of the Manhattan Project, it resonated with physicists, chemists, and scholars. The theories formulated by him and his team, along with their experiments and results, became subjects of study, discussion, and sometimes disagreement.

Scientific conferences during that period were abuzz with discussions revolving around the findings from Los Alamos. People eagerly awaited Oppenheimer's presentations not for their depth of knowledge but for the philosophical and ethical perspectives he often infused within them. His ability to bridge the gap between intricacies, like quantum mechanics and broader implications surrounding power made him a unique voice.

However, the collaborative nature of the community faced its fair share of challenges. The era of the Cold War, characterized by rooted mistrust and espionage, impacted international scientific endeavors. Given his role in the age, Oppenheimer often found himself amid these geopolitical currents. While he worked with individuals from Europe, Asia, and beyond, exchanging insights and engaging in debates, the political realities of that time meant that these interactions were frequently overshadowed by suspicion and intrigue.

As nations embarked on their programs, the line between cooperation and competition became increasingly blurry. Pursuing supremacy driven by pride and strategic considerations led to scientific breakthroughs being closely guarded secrets. Oppenheimer staunchly advocated for control over energy and disarmament but often conflicted with this secretive and competitive mindset. His calls for transparency, openness, and collaboration resonated with many within the community but also drew criticism from political and military establishments.

During Oppenheimer's era, the global scientific community mirrored world dynamics. It was a place where the pursuit of knowledge intersected with the complexities of politics, where the ideals of collaboration clashed with the demands of security, and where the potential of energy confronted the dangers of nuclear warfare. Throughout it, all, influential figures like Oppenheimer, with their brilliance, foresight, and moral compass, played a role in shaping conversations, guiding research endeavors, and ultimately determining the course of the age.

The atomic age brought discoveries and had profound implications that brought about collaboration and occasional conflicts. As nations grappled with the realities surrounding power, scientists worldwide found themselves at a juncture where knowledge, ethics, and geopolitics converged.

J. Robert Oppenheimer naturally emerged as a figure in this scientific community due to his unmatched expertise and leadership in developing atomic bombs. His work not addressed the challenges encountered during the Manhattan Project but also resonated deeply with physicists, chemists, and scholars worldwide. The theories formulated by him and his team, along with their experiments and results, became subjects of study and discussion. At times even disagreement.

In the era of conferences, there was always a buzz surrounding discussions about the latest findings from Los Alamos. People eagerly looked forward to Oppenheimer's presentations not for the depth of knowledge they offered but for the philosophical and ethical reflections he seamlessly integrated into his talks. His unique ability to connect concepts with broader philosophical implications made him a captivating voice that could delve into quantum mechanics intricacies and the wider impact of harnessing atomic power.

However, despite the atmosphere within the scientific community, challenges arose. The Cold War, characterized by mistrust and espionage, overshadowed international scientific endeavors. Given his role in shaping the age, Oppenheimer often found himself at the center of these geopolitical undercurrents. While he collaborated with researchers from Europe, Asia, and beyond to exchange insights and engage in debates, political realities at that time meant that these interactions were often riddled with suspicion and intrigue.

As nations pursued their programs, collaboration began to intermingle with competition. The race for supremacy driven by pride and strategic considerations blurred boundaries between scientific discoveries and closely guarded secrets.
Oppenheimer, a supporter of oversight of atomic energy and disarmament, often found himself in conflict with the secretive

and competitive nature of the field. While his calls for transparency, collaboration, and openness resonated with scientists, they also drew criticism from political and military authorities.

Essentially during Oppenheimer's time, the global scientific community mirrored the world. It was a space where the pursuit of knowledge intersected with realities. It was a place where collaborative ideals clashed with national security imperatives. It was an arena where the potential of energy confronted the dangers of nuclear warfare. Throughout it, all, brilliant individuals like Oppenheimer played a role in shaping discussions guiding research efforts, and ultimately determining the path of the age based on their intellect, foresight, and moral compass.

A Legacy Beyond Borders:

The impact of J. Robert Oppenheimer extended beyond the deserts of New Mexico or the academic institutions in America. His legacy, intertwined with the emergence of the age, had an influence that reached every corner of the world. Oppenheimer's work resonated universally from the streets of Hiroshima to the scientific communities in Europe, from political arenas in the Middle East to emerging voices in Africa and Latin America. His contributions to science and his considerations positioned him as a globally respected and scrutinized figure. Oppenheimer emerges not only as an exceptional physicist but also as a global citizen whose thoughts, dilemmas, and discoveries continue to mold our collective journey in this nuclear era.

CHAPTER 10: THE MAN BEHIND THE LEGEND.

Who was behind the fame, recognition, and ethical challenges associated with J. Robert Oppenheimer, the figure in energy and scientific brilliance?

To understand Oppenheimer, this chapter will go beyond his image and explore the complexity of his personal life, his connections with others, and the transformative experiences that molded him.

A Multifaceted Personality:

J. Robert Oppenheimer was a man of complexity, embodying a mix of contrasting qualities that went well beyond his scientific accomplishments. While the world admired him for his brilliance in physics, those who knew him personally were often amazed by the depth and breadth of his interests. His thirst for knowledge extended beyond laboratories and equations; it encompassed subjects from around the world and throughout history.

From studying philosophical works to appreciating contemporary Western literary masterpieces, Oppenheimer's hunger for knowledge knew no bounds. He effortlessly discussed concepts in quantum mechanics while also quoting verses from the Bhagavad Gita or delving into the intricacies of poetry. This unique combination of rigor and artistic appreciation set him apart within circles during his time. It was not unusual for colleagues and students to converse with him only to be surprised by his deep insights into topics ranging from Eastern mysticism to classical music or European art.

His multifaceted nature also revealed itself in his problem-solving approach. Oppenheimer firmly believed in the interconnectedness between disciplines. He often drew parallels between patterns and musical rhythms; made connections between principles in physics and philosophies held by ancient civilizations.

This comprehensive approach enhanced his perspectives enabling him to consider challenges from angles and often resulting in solutions.

However, this complexity of character also presented its set of difficulties. The same mind that effortlessly explored the realms of science and art frequently grappled with the implications of his work after the Manhattan Project. His deep understanding of humanity derived from his interests intensified the dilemmas he faced in the atomic age. The weight of these introspections, combined with the pressures of his life, made Oppenheimer a captivating figure who evoked both admiration and sympathy at times.

In essence, J. Robert Oppenheimer was not merely a physicist; he embodied a Renaissance spirit—a figure in the 20th century who illuminated the intersection of science, art, philosophy, and ethics. His life is a testament to the potential of spirit when curiosity is coupled with passion and intellect.

The Family Man:

In the comfort of his home away from the eye and the weight of professional duties, J. Robert Oppenheimer revealed a side of himself that he often kept hidden. As a husband and father, he embodied roles quite different from the analytical physicist known to the world.

Oppenheimer shared a multifaceted relationship with his wife, Katherine "Kitty" Oppenheimer. They engaged in pursuits together, harboring respect and affection for one another. Kitty, a biologist herself, was not Oppenheimer's partner but also his trusted confidante. Their conversations delved into topics beyond concerns exploring philosophy, art, and the ethical implications of progress. In Kitty, Oppenheimer found solace—a person who truly comprehended the intricacies of his mind and understood the burdens he carried in his heart. Their letters reflected their tender connection and profound understanding of each other's dreams and vulnerabilities.

The joys of being a parent added another layer to Oppenheimer's life. His children, Peter and Toni, received love and attention from him. Despite his demanding profession, Oppenheimer prioritized being actively involved in their lives—cherishing those moments that shape one's childhood.

Whether it involved assisting with projects engaging in banter, or introducing them to the marvels of the cosmos, he was a devoted and caring father. Peter and Toni often share memories that depict their father as someone who, despite his brilliance, took pleasure in life's joys—from family picnics to stargazing sessions to listening to music; these moments showcased Oppenheimer's dedication to his family.

However, like any individual, Oppenheimer had moments of self-reflection and uncertainty after the Manhattan Project. It was during these times that the strength of his bonds became evident. Kitty, Peter, and Toni provided him with a haven—a space where he could confront his emotions seek comfort, and gather the courage to move forward. Their constant support, understanding, and love served as the foundation Oppenheimer relied on during his trying periods.

Oppenheimer's family dynamics offered a contrasting perspective to his image. They humanized him—reminding us that behind the figure was a man with dreams, aspirations, fears, and unwavering devotion to those he cherished.

The Oppenheimer family's home walls held the memories of laughter, debates, quiet moments, and shared experiences that defined them—these glimpses into J. Robert Oppenheimer's life revealed his nature as a devoted family man.

Friendships and Mentorships:

J. Robert Oppenheimer's connections with his colleagues, students, and peers showcased his personality. While he was widely recognized as a physicist, those who knew him closely experienced his warmth, humor, and profound wisdom. He formed friendships with various people, including scientists, artists, and intellectuals. These friendships were built on conversations, mutual respect, and a shared love for learning.

One of the qualities in Oppenheimer's relationships was his concern for the well-being and development of those around him. This was particularly evident in his role as a mentor. Many young physicists who were drawn to the University of California Berkeley or the Los Alamos Laboratory sought not his expertise in physics but his guidance in navigating the intricate world of academia and research. Oppenheimer could recognize the potential in others and often encouraged his students to explore areas they hadn't previously considered. His mentorship extended beyond matters; he frequently engaged them in discussions that prompted them to ponder the broader implications of their work.

His connections with scientists such as Niels Bohr, Enrico Fermi, and Richard Feynman were characterized by admiration and a spirit of collaboration.

Oppenheimer engaged in discussions with Bohr on the philosophical foundations of quantum mechanics. Their extensive correspondence over the years offers a glimpse into the thoughts of two physicists grappling with the mysteries of the universe.

However, Oppenheimer's connections extended beyond scientists. He formed friendships with artists, writers, and political thinkers, giving him a needed break from equations and theories. These relationships broadened his perspective; allowed him to find connections between unrelated fields. Conversations at Oppenheimer's home were diverse, ranging from analyzing plays to dissecting events.

In ways, these personal connections humanized Oppenheimer. They revealed a man to the world around him—always curious and eager to learn and evolve. Late-night physics discussions, debates over meals, or moments of reflection with close friends reflected his authenticity and profound nature.

While Oppenheimer's scientific contributions hold significance, it is through these personal relationships that we gain insight into his soul.

They serve as a reminder that there was a person behind the stories who cherished connection, empathy, and the collective quest for knowledge.

The Weight of Responsibility:

The atomic age, which began with the blinding flash of the Trinity test in 1945, was not a result of scientific efforts but also owed much to Oppenheimer's ingenuity. This groundbreaking event irreversibly transformed the world, making Oppenheimer a central figure in this shift. The initial thrill of achievement soon gave way to a realization of the immense destructive power of the weapon. As the architect behind the bomb, Oppenheimer carried the weight of this realization more heavily than most.

For Oppenheimer, the bombings of Hiroshima and Nagasaki went beyond being events; they were deeply personal reckonings. In those aftermath moments, he famously quoted from the

Bhagavad Gita; "Now I am become Death, the destroyer of worlds." This reflection not acknowledged the capabilities of the bomb but also delved into a profound introspection regarding its ethical and moral implications.

While the rest of the world celebrated victory and peace in World War IIs end, Oppenheimer immersed himself in contemplation. The paradoxical experience of being hailed as a hero while grappling internally with guilt and responsibility weighed heavily on him. Friends and colleagues noticed a change in his demeanor – a somberness that hadn't been present before.

During that time, when conversing with him, our discussions often steered toward topics like philosophy, ethics, and the impact of science on shaping the future of humanity.

His subsequent push for energy regulation and his vocal opposition to developing the hydrogen bomb was largely driven by his desire to reconcile with his conscience. Oppenheimer firmly believed that scientists, having unraveled the secrets of the atom, had a duty to ensure its use. While this noble stance often placed him at odds with military authorities, it ultimately revoked his security clearance in 1954.

His trial wasn't a setback in his life but public scrutiny of his loyalty and integrity. This was an overwhelming blow for a man already grappling with dilemmas brought upon by the atomic age. Nevertheless, in the years that followed, Oppenheimer continued to speak out, educate others and advocate for an approach to power that emphasized peace and international cooperation than militarization.

When we examine J. Robert Oppenheimer's journey through the age from a perspective, it serves as a testament to the intricate nature of scientific discovery; it underscores how delicate it is to strike a balance between pursuing knowledge and fulfilling responsibilities. His narrative serves as a reminder that unique obstacles, difficult choices, and obligations accompany every significant advancement.

Passions Beyond Physics:

J. Robert Oppenheimer is widely recognized as a physicist in history. It would be an oversimplification to limit his identity to this field. He was an individual with interests that extended beyond equations and theories. Oppenheimer had an appreciation for the aspects of life, particularly the arts and humanities.

His personal library was a treasure trove of literature from languages and genres reflecting his ranging interests. From the verses of romantics to the philosophical treatises of Eastern thinkers, Oppenheimer immersed himself in worlds crafted by words. He often drew connections between the uncertainties of quantum mechanics. The ambiguities found within verses see both as avenues to explore the nature of existence and unravel the mysteries of the universe.

Music held a place in Oppenheimer's heart well. He loved compositions, particularly those by Ludwig van Beethoven and Johann Sebastian Bach, which often resonated through his home. Colleagues recall evenings where conversations seamlessly transitioned from discussions about particles to delving into the intricacies of specific musical pieces. Oppenheimer would find solace at the piano allowing his fingers to dance across the keys as he translated his emotions into melodies.

These moments, which were often personal and intimate, allowed us to catch a glimpse of a side of Oppenheimer – one that was reflective and deeply sensitive.

Oppenheimer's journeys exposed him to cultures, each contributing to his broadened perspective. He was fascinated with philosophy and frequently quoted from the Bhagavad Gita, an esteemed Hindu scripture. This attraction to Eastern thought went beyond interest; it influenced his views on life's purpose, responsibilities, and the ethical implications of his scientific endeavors. The concept of 'dharma' or righteous duty, prevalent in philosophies, deeply resonated with him in the aftermath of the atomic bombings.

Essentially Oppenheimer's passions extended beyond physics and painted a picture of someone constantly seeking knowledge not only about the world but also about their own inner self. Whether through literature, music, or philosophy, he strived to comprehend the intricacies of existence and discover significance within the interplay between science and art.

Beyond the Atomic Shadow:

J. Robert Oppenheimer's impact on history is undeniably intertwined with age. However, as we delve into his story, it becomes clear that he was much more than the "Father of the Atomic Bomb." He embodied a mix of qualities; a scientist with a poetic soul, a public figure who cherished moments of solitude, a leader faced with moral dilemmas, and a lifelong student despite being an esteemed teacher.

His multifaceted nature, influenced by interests like philosophy and classical music, paints a picture of someone constantly seeking knowledge and deeper understanding. The relationships he cultivated—be it with family, friends, or students—reveal a depth and ability to connect that extended beyond the confines of his work.

His weighty responsibilities after the Manhattan Project demonstrate his struggle to reconcile the consequences of his actions while striving for a balance between scientific progress and ethical accountability. His introspection, dilemmas, and eventual advocacy for peace and disarmament highlight the workings of a mind at the forefront of one of humanity's pivotal moments.

Understanding Oppenheimer's story reminds us that even legends are human. Their greatness is not found in what they accomplish but in their vulnerabilities, moments of self-reflection, and search for purpose. As we conclude this chapter on "The Man Behind the Legend, " let us embrace an understanding of J. Robert Oppenheimer moving beyond the overshadowing impact of the atomic era to recognize the radiant spirit that illuminated the many aspects of his remarkable life.

PSYCHOLOGICAL INSIGHTS AND PROFILE

J. Robert Oppenheimer is a name that is widely recognized for his brilliance, controversial nature, and significant role in the age. However, who was the individual beyond his image? What were the motivations, haunting experiences, and sources of inspiration that shaped him? This chapter explores different aspects of Oppenheimer's life, aiming to gain insight into the mind of one of the most mysterious figures of the 20th century.

Childhood and Formative Years: The Seeds of Complexity:

In the heart of New York City, nestled within a home, a young boy named Julius Robert Oppenheimer embarked on his journey of exploration and self-discovery. He grew up in an environment that was both affluent and intellectually stimulating. With his father's success as a textile importer and his mother's artistic talents, their home became a haven of wisdom and cultural richness. These early surroundings exposed Oppenheimer to a world of ideas that fueled his curiosity.

At an age, Robert demonstrated signs of extraordinary intellect. He possessed not an aptitude for learning but also the ability to delve deeply into matters. Oppenheimer often sought solace in books while his peers were engrossed in activities. His reading choices went beyond children's stories; he delved into literature, philosophy, and even scientific works. These early reading habits indicated the presence of a mind to unravel the intricacies of the world.

It wasn't intellectual pursuits that shaped his formative years. Young Oppenheimer possessed sensitivity and introspection traits that set him apart from others. There were moments when profound contemplation took hold of him during times. Friends and family recalled instances where he would become lost in thought, pondering questions beyond his tender age.

His unique combination of insight and emotional depth set him apart in the vibrant and diverse city of New York. His education further refined his talents. Teachers quickly recognized his spark, often commenting on his observation skills and knack for effortlessly grasping ideas. However, it wasn't excellence that defined him. Oppenheimer's formative years were also marked by a search for identity. As a young Jewish boy navigating an environment, he often wrestled with questions of faith, culture, and belonging. These early encounters with issues of identity and belonging would later shape his perspectives on society, politics, and ethics.

With its pulsing energy and diverse population, New York City played a role in shaping Oppenheimer's worldview. The city was a melting pot of ideas, cultures, and philosophies. The early 20th century witnessed transformations encompassing advancements, socio-political upheavals, and cultural revolutions. Growing up amidst such an environment exposed Oppenheimer to a multitude of perspectives. This exposure enriched his thinking process by enabling him to perceive the world not through the lens of a physicist but as a global citizen.

From the beginning, J. Robert Oppenheimer's early years were not solely focused on his emergence as a physicist; they encompassed the shaping of a complex individual. This individual ultimately alters the trajectory of history not through his achievements but also through his deep comprehension of the human experience.

The Duality of the Scientist and the Philosopher:

J. Robert Oppenheimer wasn't a physicist. He was also a thinker who sought truths beyond what could be empirically proven. His journey into the world of science went hand in hand with his exploration of philosophy and spirituality. This dual pursuit wasn't merely an endeavor; it reflected his quest to comprehend the universe and his place within it.

From attending lectures at Harvard to being part of institutions in Europe, Oppenheimer's scientific pursuits were characterized by their rigor and brilliance. He delved deeply into quantum mechanics aiming to unravel the world's mysteries. However, alongside his analytical mind, there existed a soul that yearned for existential answers. His fascination with the Bhagavad Gita, a text from India, supports this yearning. Gita's exploration of duty, righteousness, and the nature of reality deeply resonated with Oppenheimer. It provided him solace. Offered insights into the moral dilemmas he grappled with.

The interplay between Oppenheimer, as a scientist and philosopher, became most apparent in the aftermath of the Trinity test as he witnessed the mushroom cloud rising over the New Mexicos desert, marking an era defined by atomic power. Oppenheimer's response revealed much about him.

Quoting from the Gita, he uttered, "Now I have become Death, the destroyer of worlds." This statement didn't merely highlight the might of the bomb; it acknowledged the ethical implications of his work. The excitement of exploration was intertwined with the terror of its consequences.

Oppenheimer endeavored to strike a balance between these two facets that defined him throughout his life. His scientific presentations are often interwoven with contemplations. His discussions on energy encompassed both aspects and ethical considerations. This duality, while enriching, also created conflicts. The logical scientist and introspective philosopher frequently disagreed, especially when confronted with the responsibilities accompanying his groundbreaking discoveries.

In some respects, Oppenheimer's journey mirrors humanity's perpetual pursuit to reconcile knowledge with existential understanding. His life serves as a reminder that science though formidable, remains incomplete without embracing the philosophical truths that shape our existence.

The Weight of Ethical Dilemmas:

J. Robert Oppenheimer's involvement in the Manhattan Project went beyond pursuits; it was a journey filled with dilemmas. The very nature of the project aims to harness the power of the atom, raised ethical questions. As the leader of this endeavor, Oppenheimer found himself at the center of these struggles, grappling with issues beyond science and delving into matters of morality and humanity.

Initially, the urgency of winning the war justified undertaking this project. Developing a weapon became a morally complex path for the Allies in their race against Axis powers. However, as they approached its culmination, they began to grasp the potential of such a weapon. The Trinity test marked a triumph. It also prompted deep introspection for Oppenheimer. The haunting brilliance of the mushroom cloud against the backdrop of devastation served as a reminder that they had unleashed something on Pandora's box. The subsequent bombings of Hiroshima and Nagasaki further intensified these dilemmas.

The immediate devastation, followed by the lasting horrors of radiation sickness, raised moral questions about the rightness of using such a weapon on civilian populations. For Oppenheimer, these events were more than strategies; they held personal significance—each life. Every story of tragedy added to the burden of responsibility he bore. His known reflection, derived from the Bhagavad Gita – "Now I am become Death, the destroyer of worlds" – was not merely a contemplation. It embodied his struggle and a profound understanding of the consequences they had unleashed.

In the years after the war, this ethical weight became evident in Oppenheimer's advocacy for disarmament and control. The scientist who had once been at the forefront of weapon development now emerged as its outspoken critic. His speeches, lectures, and interactions were marked by a sense of urgency as he pleaded for reason in an era of power. However, these positions posed challenges for him. Oppenheimer's calls for restraint and accountability frequently put him at odds with military establishments, further complicating his complex relationship with those in power.

Essentially Oppenheimer did not view the dilemmas posed by the age as abstract concepts; rather, they were lived experiences that deeply impacted him.
They significantly shaped his perspective on the world, exerted an influence on the choices he made, and left an impact on his mindset. The gravity of these difficulties, constantly navigating the line between scientific curiosity and moral obligation, ultimately defined Oppenheimer's legacy. It positioned him as an

individual in the annals of history – a mind, a visionary thinker, and someone who possessed deep introspection.

Interactions, Relationships, and the Quest for Identity:

Oppenheimer led a life characterized by interactions and relationships that provided insights into his personality and inner world. From his days as a talented student to his later years as a prominent physicist, his relationships often reflected the internal struggles and aspirations he grappled with.

During his journey, Oppenheimer's scientific perspective was shaped by mentors. Under the guidance of figures in Europe, he not refined his understanding of quantum mechanics but also developed strong bonds with fellow physicists. These connections were built on respect and intellectual curiosity, playing a role in molding him during his formative years. However, they were not without their share of tensions. Interactions with scientists often entailed collaboration and competition due to the stakes involved in scientific breakthroughs at that time.

Beyond academia Oppenheimer's relationships also revealed insights. His relationship with his brother Frank was a blend of affection; shared intellectual pursuits. Yet it showcased differences well; while both brothers were deeply involved in physics, their paths diverged when it came to politics and ethics. Frank's overt political leanings contrasted with Robert's approach resulting in both convergences and divergences in their perspectives.

One of the relationships in Oppenheimer's life was with Jean Tatlock, a psychiatrist who held communist sympathies. Their relationship was characterized by affection and ideological differences, showcasing Oppenheimer's struggles. With her beliefs and emotional depth, Tatlock challenged and complemented Oppenheimer. Although their relationship was relatively brief, it impacted him as it shaped his perspectives on politics, war, and the moral implications of his work.

In the sphere, Oppenheimer's leadership role in the Manhattan Project brought him into contact with an array of scientists, engineers, and military personnel. These interactions were filled with contrasts. On the one hand, a shared mission fostered collaboration and mutual respect among the project members. On the hand, inevitable clashes arose due to differences in ego approaches to work and visions for the future—the dynamic between Oppenheimer and General Leslie Groves. The leader of the project exemplified this interplay. While both men were driven by urgency, their contrasting viewpoints on secrecy control over information dissemination and post-war implications of weaponry often led to conflicts.

Throughout his life journey, Oppenheimer's interactions and relationships served as reflections of his search for identity. They emphasized the contrasting aspects of his personality. The scientist and the philosopher, the leader and the team player, the public figure, and the private person. Every connection, whether personal or work-related, contributed to his character establishing him as one of the mysterious figures of the 20th century.

The Trials: A Psychological Maelstrom:

The security clearance hearings in 1954 impacted J. Robert Oppenheimer, going beyond bureaucratic procedures. It became a crucible of professional anguish for him. The very essence of his identity, shaped by years of commitment to science and service to his country, was laid bare and scrutinized in the open. Each question asked and doubt raised wasn't about his affiliations or potential security risks; it delved deep into the core of who he was and what he stood for.

Oppenheimer once hailed as the leader of the Manhattan Project, found himself in hostile territory. The hearing room, filled with officials and an unwelcoming atmosphere, transformed into an arena where his past decisions, associations, and personal conversations were meticulously examined and judged. Friends and colleagues he had known for years were summoned as witnesses blurring the boundaries between relationships and professional matters further. Every testimony provided—whether against him—added layers to the turmoil that engulfed him.

Yet beyond the recollections of facts and testimonies presented during those hearings, a sense of betrayal weighed heavily on Oppenheimer's heart. The nation he had faithfully served throughout his life questioned his loyalty and integrity—the institutions he had dedicated himself to casting doubt upon him. This trial was not a test of his actions but his character. The distinction between Oppenheimer, the scientist, and Oppenheimer, the individual, started to blur as time passed. Each night after the hearings ended, he grappled with a self-image, trying to reconcile who he believed he was and how he was portrayed in that room.

The hearings also raised questions for Oppenheimer. Questions about loyalty, the coexistence of beliefs and professional duties, and particularly the cost of truth in an era marked by political paranoia and Cold War tensions. These questions were not relevant to the context of the hearings. It also reflected the broader dilemmas faced by intellectuals and scientists during that time.

After the hearings having his security clearance revoked wasn't a setback in his career; it symbolized a loss of his identity. The confident and charismatic leader who once represented Los Alamos was replaced by someone grappling with disillusionment and introspection. However, during this period of crisis, Oppenheimer's resilience remained evident. Although scarred by the hearings, he continued to engage with science, policy, and society, albeit with a thoughtful approach.

By exploring this phase of Oppenheimer's life, we gain a deeper understanding of the man himself and a glimpse into the complex dynamics between science, politics, and personal identity during mid 20th century. The challenges faced by J. Robert Oppenheimer act as a reminder of the vulnerabilities and intricacies that even brilliant minds encounter.

Legacy: The Final Reconciliation:

As the sun started to go down on J. Robert Oppenheimer's life, the world around him experienced changes. The era of energy in which he had played a role was now in full swing, with nations racing to harness its power. However, for Oppenheimer, these years were less about events and more about a journey of reconciliation and self-reflection.

The recognition he received in his years, including the Enrico Fermi Award, was not only an acknowledgment of his scientific contributions; it also symbolized society's desire to bring closure to a chapter marked by suspicion and betrayal. While these honors brought him satisfaction, they also evoked melancholy. They served as reminders of the path he had walked—from being hailed as a hero to being accused of treason and celebrated as a visionary once again.

Beyond the acclaim, Oppenheimer's final years were characterized by deep introspection. The man who had once stood at the forefront of breakthroughs now grappled with the moral implications of his work. The bombings of Hiroshima and Nagasaki had deeply shaken him and continued to cast shadows over his thoughts. He would often contemplate the balance between curiosity and moral responsibility, questioning the very nature of progress and its associated costs.

Throughout this period, his interactions with colleagues, young physicists, and the general public were tinged with nostalgia and caution. He discussed the marvels of discovery while also expressing concerns about the dangers of ambition. In ways, he served as a bridge between the world and the new, representing both the promises and pitfalls of the atomic age.

Yet amidst this self-reflection, there was also a sense of peace—a coming to terms with his decisions and choices. In his years, Oppenheimer seemed to have found solace in recognizing his legacy. He acknowledged that while he had played a role in unleashing power, he had also ignited discussions on its responsible usage. Within this realization lay a semblance of redemption.

When future generations look back at history, J. Robert Oppenheimer will be remembered not for his brilliance but also his humanity. His life—characterized by brilliance intertwined with contradictions—is a testament to the nature of existence. As we look back on his impact, it serves as a reminder that genuine greatness is not only measured by accomplishments but also by the capacity to ask questions, reflect inwardly, and ultimately find common ground.

Unraveling the Enigma:

J. Robert Oppenheimer remains a figure in the records of history. Exploring his profile reveals a man with contradictions, a scientist with a philosophical soul, a leader burdened by ethical dilemmas, and a public figure who grappled with personal struggles at his very core. His life, characterized by accomplishments and deep introspection, reminds him of the intricacies that define the human spirit. As we conclude this chapter on Oppenheimer's world, we gain an understanding and admiration for the man behind the legend – someone multifaceted whose legacy continues to inspire and challenge us.

CHAPTER 11: LEGACY FOR A NEW GENERATION:

Few individuals in history have had an impact as J. Robert Oppenheimer. His scientific achievements, role in leading an endeavor, and subsequent contemplation of his work's ethical implications have left an enduring imprint on the world. However, what does Oppenheimer's legacy signify for the generation? How do today's youth perceive this figure? How do his life and accomplishments resonate in our contemporary era?

The Scientific Maverick:

J. Robert Oppenheimer's journey in the world of science was truly extraordinary. He possessed a curiosity and an unwavering desire for knowledge. From his days, he demonstrated a talent for asking probing questions and unraveling the mysteries of the universe. His academic pursuits, starting at Harvard and continuing in institutions, were not simply about absorbing existing information but pushing the boundaries of what was already known.

During the atmosphere of the 1920s, Oppenheimer found himself at the forefront of quantum mechanics—a field revolutionizing our comprehension of the microscopic realm. Collaborating with figures like Max Born, he delved deeply into wave functions, matrix mechanics, and the probabilistic nature of quantum phenomena. Yet what distinguished Oppenheimer wasn't his expertise; his ability to integrate various branches of physics, uncovering connections and insights that often eluded his peers.

Upon returning to the United States and assuming positions at Caltech and Berkeley, Oppenheimer dedicated himself to nurturing generations of physicists. His lectures became legendary not for their content but for his exceptional delivery. Oppenheimer possessed a talent for simplifying ideas into easily understandable concepts challenging his students to think critically, question assumptions and embark on intellectual exploration. He created an atmosphere that valued rigor, encouraging debates, discussions, and, most importantly, original thought.

However, what truly defined Oppenheimer's journey was his approach to the field. For him, physics was not a subject limited to equations and experiments. It was intricately connected to philosophy, literature, and the wider human experience. He often drew parallels between the text of Bhagavad Gita and modern physics by quoting from it. This interdisciplinary perspective made him more than a physicist; he became a polymath who bridged the gap between science and the humanities.

Throughout history, numerous individuals have been recognized for their contributions, discoveries, and innovations. Oppenheimer's impact as a trailblazer is not solely based on his accomplishments but also his approach to the discipline. He serves as a reminder that, at its essence, science is rooted in endeavors driven by curiosity, passion, and an unwavering determination to comprehend the vastness of our universe.

The Ethical Conundrum:

J. Robert Oppenheimer's exploration of the age provides a thought-provoking examination of the challenges that often accompany groundbreaking scientific progress. The very nature of his work culminating in the development of the bomb raised questions about the moral obligations of scientists and the potential consequences associated with their discoveries.

The bombings of Hiroshima and Nagasaki were not military events; they were transformative occurrences that forever altered the ethical landscape of scientific exploration. The immediate devastation and the long-term effects of radiation presented a question; Just because humanity can create something, does it mean we should? Oppenheimer himself grappled with this dilemma. His reflection drawing from the Bhagavad Gita, "Now I am become Death, the destroyer of worlds," captured his internal conflict. It served as a realization of the power and devastating potential that scientific knowledge could unleash.

This ethical quandary extended beyond the aftermath of those bombings. As we entered an era dominated by Cold War tensions, nations competed fervently in an arms race to develop potent nuclear weaponry. Oppenheimer's support for disarmament and international control over energy was grounded in his firm belief that humanity must exercise caution and wisdom when confronted with such tremendous power. However, some critics disagreed with his position. Many saw his stance as idealistic. They argued that nations should arm themselves with the powerful weapons available to counter existential threats.

Nevertheless, Oppenheimer's reflections on ethics still hold relevance in today's world, where rapid advancements in technology constantly push the boundaries of what's achievable. Modern science presents immense potential from engineering to intelligence while raising substantial ethical dilemmas. Oppenheimer's life serves as a reminder that every scientific endeavor carries implications, no matter how noble its intentions may be. It highlights the importance of self-reflection, open dialogue, and ethical considerations when pursuing knowledge.

In some respects, Oppenheimer's ethical journey mirrors the wider societal discourse on the role of science in our lives. This ongoing debate raises thought-provoking questions about accountability, responsibility, and the true nature of wielding knowledge. As we reflect upon Oppenheimer's legacy, it becomes clear that his contributions extend beyond physics into examining the aspects surrounding scientific exploration.

The Advocate for Peace:

The contributions of J. Robert Oppenheimer to the field of physics are unquestionable. Equally significant is his transformation into an advocate for peace during the atomic age. Although the bombings of Hiroshima and Nagasaki marked the end of World War II, they also ushered in an era filled with tensions and an arms race that threatened global stability. Aware of the consequences resulting from these events, Oppenheimer found himself at the forefront of discussions regarding the future use of nuclear weapons and energy.

Having witnessed firsthand the power of bombs, Oppenheimer came to a profound realization; it was no longer viable to consider atomic energy solely as a weapon. Instead, he envisioned a future where nations would collaborate on energy for peaceful purposes. This vision was not idealism; it stemmed from his understanding of the complexities and responsibilities of atomic discoveries.

Oppenheimer's call for cooperation in all technology-related matters did not always receive widespread support, particularly within the politically charged atmosphere of Cold War tensions. Nevertheless, he remained resolute in his belief that diplomacy and dialogue were crucial in preventing escalation. His efforts extended beyond advocacy. He actively engaged in conferences, discussions, and initiatives to promote disarmament and establish frameworks to oversee atomic energy.

However, Oppenheimer's stance went beyond advocating for disarmament; it aimed to redefine the narrative surrounding energy. He aimed to shift the conversation from fear and distrust to hope and collaboration. According to him, the atomic age presented humanity with an opportunity; to rise above rivalries and work together for the betterment of all. This vision was not solely focused on preventing conflicts but on creating a world where atomic energy could be utilized for progress, including advancements in medicine and power generation.

One cannot contemplate Oppenheimer's role as an advocate for peace. Be impressed by his dedication. Here was a man who played a part in developing the most destructive weapon in history, yet he devoted the latter portion of his life to ensuring that such weapons would never be used again. His journey, from being recognized as the "Father of the Atomic Bomb" to becoming a champion of peace, highlights the intricacies of experience and serves as a reminder of the responsibilities associated with knowledge and power.

The Human Behind the Legend:

J. Robert Oppenheimer, often recognized for his accomplishments and leadership roles, possessed a human essence. His life embodied the nature of the experience, characterized by moments of great triumph and deep despair. Beyond his pursuits, lectures, and involvement in politics, Oppenheimer was a man of profound introspection, vulnerability, and emotional depth.

Although born into privilege, Oppenheimer's formative years were marked by a thirst for knowledge that extended beyond science. He was equally captivated by literature, poetry, and philosophy. His fondness for English literature and his ability to quote from the Bhagavad Gita demonstrated his quest for answers not only in the empirical world but also within the realms of human thought and spirituality. This fusion of reasoning with contemplation significantly influenced Oppenheimer's worldview.

His personal life also reflected complexity. Both familial and romantic relationships were approached with the intensity and introspection he brought to his work. The joys of fatherhood, the challenges within marriage dynamics, and navigating friendships amidst the high-stakes world of research all contributed to shaping his multifaceted persona. Each relationship and interaction left a lasting impression, shaping man much as any scientific pursuit.

Oppenheimer faced challenges during the infamous AEC hearings, which peeled back the layers of his legendary status and revealed his human side. Stripped of his security clearance and confronted with allegations and suspicions, Oppenheimer's resilience was put to the test. Yet, in those times, his humanity shone brightly. His composed defense, moments of vulnerability, and unwavering commitment to his beliefs showcased a man of character and integrity.

One of the reflections of Oppenheimer's humanity was witnessed in his reaction to the detonation of the atomic bomb. The contrast between achievement and profound moral implications resulted in one of history's iconic statements. Drawing from the Bhagavad Gita Oppenheimer's words. "Now I am become Death, the destroyer of worlds." He encapsulated the turmoil he experienced, grappling with dilemmas and bearing the weighty responsibility he carried.

To truly comprehend J. Robert Oppenheimer, it is essential to look beyond his accolades, achievements, and controversies. At his core existed a man navigating life's complexities—love, morality, identity, striving to make sense of everything. His narrative is a reminder that tales, regardless of their grandeur, ultimately embody the essence of humanity.

Echoes of Oppenheimer in the Modern Era:

J. Robert Oppenheimer's impact extends beyond records and scientific research. It resonates within the halls of academia, ethical think tanks, and the aspirations of today's youth. His life showcases achievements and deep self-reflection, serving as a guiding light for the generation as they navigate the complexities of the 21st century.

Oppenheimer personifies a pursuit of knowledge while remaining acutely aware of the responsibilities of discovery. His story emphasizes the connection between science and ethics—a message that holds great significance in an era of rapid technological progress and global challenges.

For today's youth, Oppenheimer's journey imparts lessons. It underscores the significance of learning, highlights the importance of considerations in all endeavors, and reinforces the resilience required to overcome adversity. Above all, it emphasizes that introspection and personal growth are aspects of being human.

As we reflect on Oppenheimer's legacy for generations, we are reminded not of his timeless contributions but also their universal relevance in our lives. In his reflections on his ideas and actions, we discover a guide for a future shaped by knowledge, morality, and empathy.

YOUTH PERSPECTIVES AND MODERN REFLECTIONS:

Few individuals in history have had such an impact as J. Robert Oppenheimer. His scientific achievements, his role as a leader during a project for humanity, and his reflections on the implications of his work have made him a subject of study and admiration for many generations. However, it is interesting to consider how the new generation, born after the Manhattan Project and the Cold War, perceives Oppenheimer. What lessons do they learn from his life? How do they interpret his legacy in today's world?

The Digital Age and Rediscovering Oppenheimer:

In today's age of technology, our approach to history has transformed. The life and legacy of J. Robert Oppenheimer, which used to be limited to textbooks and academic journals, now resonate strongly with a generation that heavily relies on platforms for learning and discovery. The internet, with its collection of information, has made the study of figures more accessible to everyone allowing for a more comprehensive and multifaceted understanding of their contributions.

For people, their first introduction to Oppenheimer may come from sources like YouTube documentaries, interactive online lectures, or discussions on forums. These digital platforms provide an immersive experience by incorporating visuals, animations, and expert insights. They offer information and foster a deeper emotional connection with the subject matter. When watching footage of Oppenheimer discussing the consequences of the bomb, viewers can truly grasp the emotional weight behind his words, interpret his subtle expressions and understand the historical context – leaving a lasting impact.

Additionally, the interactive nature of this era encourages community engagement and collective exploration.

Online discussion forums, social media platforms, and academic networks have become gathering places where enthusiasts, scholars, and curious minds come together to discuss and analyze the life and work of Oppenheimer. These platforms encourage perspectives fostering a comprehensive understanding of

Oppenheimer's impact. For example, a student from India might offer insights into the consequences of the bomb. At the same time, a historian from Europe could shed light on the socio-political context during Oppenheimer's era. This worldwide exchange of ideas through means enriches the narrative and provides a holistic view of Oppenheimer's contributions.

Furthermore, in this era that prioritizes accessibility, individuals from backgrounds can now explore the intricacies of Oppenheimer's scientific achievements. Complex theories, research papers, and academic discussions that were once considered obscure are now presented in formats to reach a broader audience. Interactive simulations, visual representations, and expert-led webinars make complex concepts more approachable for those without a physics background to appreciate Oppenheimer's brilliance.

In summary, the digital age has revitalized the study of figures like Oppenheimer by creating opportunities for engagement and understanding.

Oppenheimer's remarkable legacy demonstrates the impact of advancements on our interaction with history. It has revolutionized how we perceive and engage with the past transforming it into an interactive field. Today his insights and reflections remain just as meaningful as they were years ago, showcasing the enduring power of the digital medium in connecting us to our historical roots.

Oppenheimer: The Reluctant Hero:

J. Robert Oppenheimer's legacy combines brilliance, leadership, and deep introspection. While his scientific accomplishments position him among the physicists of all time, his struggle with morality and ethics truly distinguishes him. Many view Oppenheimer as the epitome of a hero. Someone thrust into greatness but constantly wrestling with the weight of their actions.

His exceptional leadership during the Manhattan Project cannot be overstated. Guiding a team comprising scientists, engineers, and workers, he brought together talents to achieve what many believed impossible. The atomic bomb, an awe-inspiring display of engineering prowess, is a testament to ingenuity. However, its creation was not without its side. The bombings of Hiroshima and Nagasaki marked the end of World War II. It also unleashed a magnitude of destruction upon humanity. The haunting images of devastation, stories of loss, and profound implications ushering in the age weighed heavily on Oppenheimer's conscience.

Oppenheimer stood at a crossroads in the aftermath of war and amidst celebrations for the victory achieved. He began questioning the consequences stemming from his work. His known reflection citing the Bhagavad Gita, "Now I have become Death, the destroyer of worlds," perfectly captured his turmoil. It recognized the nature of scientific exploration—the potential for creation and destruction.

During this period of self-reflection, Oppenheimer transformed from a physicist into an advocate for disarmament and control. His speeches, lectures, and writings from this time reveal a sense of responsibility and a determination to ensure that atomic power would be used for purposes. However, he faced challenges in his advocacy efforts. Oppenheimer's past connections and his calls for disarmament made him a controversial figure in circles. The revocation of his security clearance in 1954 served as a reminder of the turbulent relationship between science, ethics, and politics.

Nevertheless, despite his difficulties, Oppenheimer's legacy as an unwilling hero persists. To people, he epitomizes the scientist—curious brilliant, and motivated by an innate desire to comprehend the universe. Yet he also embodies the aspect of science—the introspection it requires, the dilemmas it presents, and the constant pursuit of finding equilibrium between discovery and responsibility.

In an evolving world driven by progress, Oppenheimer's voyage is a timeless testament, to the importance of ethics, in our pursuits.

The Ethical Scientist: A Role Model for Today:

J. Robert Oppenheimer's place in history is remarkable not for his exceptional intelligence and accomplishments but also his deep contemplation of ethical issues. As science and technology continue to advance, the ethical aspects of research and innovation have gained importance. Oppenheimer's experiences provide insights into the relationship between scientific progress and moral responsibility.

Under Oppenheimer's leadership, the Manhattan Project showcased creativity and determination. However, this achievement also posed a dilemma. The atomic bomb, a breakthrough, carried immense destructive potential. Oppenheimer's subsequent reflections on the consequences of his work reveal a sense of accountability. His known quote from the Bhagavad Gita, "Now I am become Death, the destroyer of worlds," uttered after the Trinity test, symbolizes the ethical considerations he grappled with.

For aspiring scientists and researchers today, Oppenheimer's ethical journey holds significance. The moral implications are vast and intricate in an era where artificial intelligence, genetic engineering, and other cutting-edge technologies are making strides. Each discovery or innovation brings both promises of improvement and risks of misuse.

The life of Oppenheimer reminds us of the importance of considering ethics in endeavors regardless of how groundbreaking they may be.

Oppenheimer's post-war years were characterized by his advocacy for disarmament and an open approach to atomic energy at an international level. This demonstrates scientists' role in shaping policies and engaging in discussions. He firmly believed that scientists have a responsibility to guide and inform conversations due to their understanding of the implications of their work. This belief holds relevance today as we face challenges such as climate change, data privacy, and bioethics. Scientists possess knowledge that equips them to shape ethical policies.

In essence, J. Robert Oppenheimer's legacy as a scientist guides today's generation. It emphasizes the idea that along with power comes responsibility. As torchbearers of progress, researchers and innovators must consistently consider the ethical aspects of their work, ensuring that scientific advancements remain grounded in moral values while continuing to move forward steadfastly.

The Global Perspective: Oppenheimer in a Connected World:

In today's world, which's highly interconnected, the influence of J. Robert Oppenheimer goes beyond boundaries. His contributions to science and his involvement in the creation of the bomb have made a lasting impact on history, establishing him as a figure of international significance. For the younger generation growing up in an era where information seamlessly travels around the globe, Oppenheimer is not a physicist but also a worldwide symbol whose work has had far-reaching consequences beyond just the United States.

This global perspective on Oppenheimer's legacy is enriched by interpretations and understandings from cultures and nations. In Europe, for example, he is often seen within the community of the early 20th century that included renowned figures like Albert Einstein, Niels Bohr, and Werner Heisenberg. The collaborative spirit of that time, characterized by exchanges of ideas and knowledge across borders, contrasts the Cold War period when science often became entangled in geopolitical rivalries.

In Asia, in countries such as Japan that have directly experienced the devastating effects of weapons, Oppenheimer's legacy brings forth a mix of admiration for his scientific brilliance and reflection on the ethical responsibilities scientists bear. His reflections after the war and his efforts to promote disarmament deeply resonate in these regions serving as a reminder of the profound consequences that scientific discoveries can have.

Oppenheimer's life and work have become study subjects in institutions and discussion forums worldwide. Historians, political scientists, ethicists, and physicists all explore aspects of his legacy from their perspectives. These diverse interpretations, made possible by exchanging ideas in today's age, enhance our understanding of Oppenheimer and the intricate interplay between science, ethics, and politics during the 20th century.

Furthermore, as global challenges such as climate change, cybersecurity threats, and bioethical dilemmas take stage, Oppenheimer's life serves as a blueprint for collaboration. His story highlights the significance of transcending interests and working together for the good. The interconnected challenges we face in the 21st century demand comprehensive solutions. In this context, gaining a perspective on Oppenheimer's legacy offers insights.

Although J. Robert Oppenheimer's contributions were grounded in a time and place, their impact remains timeless and universal.

When we consider his impact on a scale, we gain an understanding of the difficulties and obligations that accompany scientific exploration. This makes him a figure who remains significant in our interconnected world.

Legacy Reimagined:

J. Robert Oppenheimer's legacy is not a relic of the past. It continues to evolve and resonate with each new generation. His life was marked by achievements and deep reflections, providing relevant lessons in today's fast-paced world.

Oppenheimer stands out in the history of science not for his contributions to physics but also his profound philosophical contemplations on the consequences of his work. While the atomic bomb showcased brilliance, it also posed ethical dilemmas. Oppenheimer's subsequent musings on the responsibilities of scientists have become a guiding light for today's researchers, who often grapple with complex questions amidst groundbreaking innovations. His journey serves as a reminder that science, despite its glory and potential, must always be guided by a sense of conscience.

For the youth of the century, Oppenheimer's story is particularly captivating. In a world where information's abundant and boundaries are increasingly blurred, they find inspiration in his ability to navigate situations with grace, introspection, and his propensity to question and reflect upon. Considering broader societal implications offers them a blueprint for ethically conscious engagement with the world.

Oppenheimer's impact extends beyond his accomplishments. His legacy serves as a motivation for action, urging us to pursue knowledge with passion and approach discoveries responsibly.

Oppenheimer's global outlook, interactions with figures from fields, and emphasis on collaboration highlight the significance of interconnectedness. His approach is a valuable model in our world, where challenges are increasingly intricate, and solutions demand collective efforts. It reminds us that progress in science or any other domain relies on collaboration that transcends borders and disciplines.

When we contemplate the legacy of Oppenheimer, we cannot help but marvel at its nature. It is a testament to celebrating knowledge pursuit, emphasizing considerations, and advocating for collaboration. As we navigate the complexities and opportunities of our time, the life and work of J. Robert Oppenheimer serve as guiding beacons that illuminate our path toward curiosity, responsibility, and collective advancement.

CONCLUSION: REFLECTING ON THE LIFE AND LEGACY OF J. ROBERT OPPENHEIMER

As we come to the end of this exploration into the life of J. Robert Oppenheimer, we find ourselves at an intersection where history, science, ethics, and human nature converge. The preceding chapters have taken us on a journey through time, delving deeply into the workings of a man called the "Father of the Atomic Bomb." However, what becomes evident is that Oppenheimer's identity extends beyond being a physicist or project leader; he was a multifaceted individual whose life was filled with remarkable achievements, daunting challenges, introspection, and moral quandaries.

In Chapter 1, we explored Oppenheimer's years to understand the factors that contributed to his intellect. Through anecdotes and tales showcasing his prowess, we gained insight into the formative experiences that shaped his intellectual trajectory. His childhood was characterized by curiosity and an unquenchable thirst for knowledge—a foundation that paved the way for his later contributions to science.

Chapter 2 provided a behind-the-scenes look at the Manhattan Project—an environment with high-pressure circumstances during wartime research. Through accounts shared within these pages, we were able to experience both the challenges faced and moments of revelation that ultimately led to the creation of one of humanity's most significant technological advancements—the atomic bomb.

The project carried a weight of responsibility with dilemmas and far-reaching implications that were deeply felt.

Chapter 3 focused on Oppenheimer's navigation through a maze. As we explored discussions and debates, we grappled with the aspects of scientific discoveries. The age of power presented both promises and dangers, compelling society and Oppenheimer himself to face questions about the role of science in shaping our future.

In Chapter 4, we were transported to the realm of the Cold War, where tales of espionage and intrigue unfolded. Oppenheimer's life became intertwined with the tensions of that era, marked by suspicion, surveillance, and political maneuvering. Real-life stories of spies highlighted the interplay between science, politics, and national security.

Chapter 5 delved into Oppenheimer's collaborations and rivalries within the field. The mid-20th century was a period for physics filled with innovation and competition. Through reconstructions, we witnessed the dynamics between Oppenheimer and his contemporaries—understanding both their camaraderie and conflicts that shaped the landscape.

In Chapter 6, an array of depictions showcased how Oppenheimer has been portrayed in culture. From films to literature, his legacy has left a mark on our consciousness—a testament to society's enduring fascination with the man himself and the mythical persona surrounding him.

Chapter 7 showcased the prominence of the scholar and the teacher. We gained a portrayal of Oppenheimer as an educator, mentor, and perpetual learner through guest essays and reflections. His profound influence on students, colleagues, and the wider academic community left an enduring impact on physics.

Moving on to Chapter 8, we delved into the challenges, hardships, and political dynamics that shaped the phases of Oppenheimer's life. The AEC hearing took the stage as a courtroom drama that underscored the tensions between rights, national security concerns, and political agendas.

Chapter 9 allowed us to trace Oppenheimer's impact through maps while comprehending his role on the international atomic stage. His advocacy for disarmament, fostering cooperation, and promoting applications of atomic energy resonated across borders.

In Chapter 10, we gained insights into the man behind the legend. By delving into his psyche, we explored the intricacies of his aspirations and internal conflicts that defined Oppenheimer's nature.

Lastly, Chapter 11 turned our gaze toward the future by capturing youth perspectives and contemporary reflections on Oppenheimer's legacy. His life story and contributions inspire generations while provoking contemplation and intellectual discourse.

To put it simply, J. Robert Oppenheimer's life encapsulated aspects of the century—its aspirations, anxieties, achievements, and ethical dilemmas.

As we wrap up this journey, we admire the individual, the scholar, and the iconic figure. His tale acts as a reminder of the influence of wisdom, the obligations it brings, and the everlasting pursuit of enlightenment.

THE END

References

Bird, K., & Sherwin, M. J. (2005). American Prometheus: The Triumph and Tragedy of J. Robert Oppenheimer. Vintage.

Rhodes, R. (1986). The Making of the Atomic Bomb. Simon & Schuster.

Kelly, C. C. (Ed.). (2007). The Manhattan Project: The Birth of the Atomic Bomb in the Words of Its Creators, Eyewitnesses, and Historians. Black Dog & Leventhal.

Conant, J. (2005). 109 East Palace: Robert Oppenheimer and the Secret City of Los Alamos. Simon & Schuster.

Herken, G. (2002). Brotherhood of the Bomb: The Tangled Lives and Loyalties of Robert Oppenheimer, Ernest Lawrence, and Edward Teller. Henry Holt and Co.

Bernstein, J. (2009). Oppenheimer: Portrait of an Enigma. Ivan R. Dee.

Monk, R. (2012). Robert Oppenheimer: A Life Inside the Center. Doubleday.

Bethe, H. A. (1997). The Road from Los Alamos. American Institute of Physics.

Cassidy, D. C. (2005). J. Robert Oppenheimer and the American Century. Pi Press.

Polenberg, R. (2002). In the Matter of J. Robert Oppenheimer: The Security Clearance Hearing. Cornell University Press.

Oppenheimer movie 2023, written and directed by Christopher Nolan

A MESSAGE FROM THE PUBLISHER:

Are you enjoying the book? We would love to hear your thoughts!

Many readers do not know how hard reviews are to come by and how much they help a publisher. We would be incredibly grateful if you could take just a few seconds to write a brief review on Amazon, even if it's just a few sentences!

Please go here and find the book to leave a quick review:

https://amazon.com/review/create-review?&asin=B0CF47FMBK

or to this short link:

https://ACCESS.TOP/review-oppenheimer

We would greatly appreciate it if you could take the time to post your review of the book and share your thoughts with the community. If you have enjoyed the book, please let us know what you loved the most about it and if you would recommend it to others. Your feedback is valuable to us, and it helps us to improve our services and continue to offer high-quality literature to our readers.

Made in the USA
Coppell, TX
19 September 2023

21768305R00128